KNACK
MAKE IT EASY

PIANO
FOR EVERYONE

KNACK

PIANO
FOR EVERYONE

A Step-by-Step Guide to Notes, Chords, and Playing Basics

Margaret Ann Martin

Photographs by Keira Schwarz

KNACK
MAKE IT EASY

Guilford, Connecticut
An imprint of Globe Pequot Press

To buy books in quantity for corporate use
or incentives, call **(800) 962-0973**
or e-mail **premiums@GlobePequot.com**.

Editor in Chief: Maureen Graney
Editor: Katie Benoit
Cover Design: Paul Beatrice, Bret Kerr
Interior Design: Paul Beatrice
Layout: Kevin Mak
Music Notation by Darryl Gregory
Cover photos by (left to right) © shutterstock, © dreamstime, © dreamstime, © dreamstime
Back cover: © shutterstock
Interior photos by Keira Schwarz with the exception of p. 16 (left): Department of Music, University of California, Berkeley; p. 17 (left): Department of Music, University of California, Berkeley

Library of Congress Cataloging-in-Publication Data is available on file.

ISBN 978-1-59921-781-9

The following manufacturer/name appearing in *Knack Piano for Everyone* is a trademark: iPod®

Printed in China

10 9 8 7 6 5 4 3 2 1

For Bill, without whom I could never have done this.

CONTENTS

INTRODUCTION

Playing the piano can be simultaneously rewarding, frustrating, and enjoyable. Learning to play is a gradual process requiring considerable patience, but if you persevere you will experience many rewards. You'll feel the joy of having the melody and accompaniment in your two hands, and you'll feel a terrific sense of accomplishment.

Examining the history of keyboard instruments reveals many wonderful innovations. Before the piano appeared about 1720, the harpsichord had prominence. The mechanism for that instrument was a string plucked by a sharpened and shaped quill affixed to a "jack," which was placed at a right angle to the key. When you pressed the key the jack moved up and the quill plucked the string.

The harpsichord was made larger and louder by adding a second keyboard (and therefore another set of strings), sometimes a pedal keyboard, and for a single-keyboard instrument, a second set of strings tuned an octave higher. But no matter how you struck the keys, the tone did not change, and the sound decayed quickly.

With the invention of the *fortepiano* (Italian for "loud/soft"), as it was originally called, the sound of the keyboard changed. You could produce both soft and loud sounds by touching the keys with varying degrees of weight. The piano eventually developed into the large instrument of today, with 88 keys (rather than 35), an iron frame (rather than a wooden one), and a complicated mechanism that uses felt hammers to strike the strings, dampers that cut off the sound as soon as the finger releases the key, an escapement action to let the hammer bounce away from the string as soon as it is struck, and pedals that control the dampers and regulate a softer sound. The development of the piano is a fascinating study!

Why learn the piano? For one, the arrangement of black and white keys helps first-time players learn music notation more easily. That same arrangement of keys is also a tactile way to learn music. You can play all styles of music on the piano. The basics of playing and reading music can be applied to popular music, classical music, jazz, or any genre. Then there is the ensemble aspect; you can play alone or with another pianist, or with other instrumentalists. If you enjoy singing, you can accompany yourself on the piano; or you can accompany other singers.

I have observed the order in which musical learning takes place. My mentors and inspirations have taught me that you cannot play scales until you understand what a half step and a whole step are, and that you cannot play any kind of music successfully until you understand the building blocks for that music. My experience with many different types of music has taught me that the building blocks for all those different types are the same. Most important, I have learned that listening to music and hearing what goes into the making of the music is the best instructor.

In my career as a pianist, I have enjoyed accompanying singers, violinists, cellists, flutists, clarinetists, percussionists, and trumpet players. There is a special joy in playing with each of these instruments, and with groups of instrumentalists. Just as special is the experience of playing with other pianists, in duet, or in duo-piano format. The process of working out how and why to play a passage a certain way is very rewarding, and the prize is a public performance in which all the musical elements, and the way in which you have rehearsed them, come to light.

To instruct students, no matter what age, in this same process, has been even more instructive to me. As a teacher

It has been a revelation to put into writing the aspects of music that I teach. Teaching classes in beginning piano basics for adults has been most helpful, because I see the variety of paces at which adults learn. Usually because of their experiences with music, or lack of experiences with music, they learn at vastly different rates. Hopefully this book will be fulfilling to all types of learners. If a student needs to take time over a specific aspect of piano, he/she can stop in a certain place in the book and work it out slowly and thoroughly. If a person can read music and wants to go on to the next step, that person can easily skip to a part of the book that will challenge him/her. Knowing how much information to convey at certain times has forced me to think in detail about the data needed to learn the piano on one's own.

I hope that I have shown how much joy there is in making music, and how much joy there is in learning about piano, about music, and about practicing in order to make it all come together.

What do you need in order to learn to play piano?

1. You need an overwhelming desire to express yourself musically. Some people desire to sing; some people desire to dance; you want to play the piano.

2. You need a piano, or an electric keyboard.

3. You need a pedal with that keyboard. Often an electric piano comes with a little square pedal that slides on the floor or carpet (you have to tape it down!). I purchased a pedal that looks and feels like a real piano pedal, and it is definitely worth the extra money.

4. You need the ability to listen. You need to listen intelligently to different kinds of music, and you need to listen intelligently to your own playing.

5. You need the ability to make time for yourself. You need a block of time each day in which you can focus on learning to play the piano.

6. Most of all, you need patience. Even for the most talented, the ability to play a piece of music takes lots of time. You must exercise your fingers so that they become equally facile, and this takes time and daily work. All the fantasizing, all the thinking about how to play and how to read music, does not substitute for daily practicing.

As a child I sang as much as I played piano. I believe that has added to my ability to play music on an instrument. If you do not sing, I encourage you to do so. I hear you saying, "But I don't sing." It doesn't matter if you cannot carry a tune. It doesn't matter if you have the smallest range (between

your lowest note and your highest note). It doesn't matter what kind of music you sing. Just sing! Sing in the shower, sing along with your iPod, sing along with the radio.

Why sing? Because you naturally let the music flow when you sing. One of the difficult things about learning to play the piano is the stop-and-start syndrome as you learn to read the notes. If you can imitate the flow of music from your singing (it doesn't matter how you sing or how badly you sing, the music still flows), it helps your playing to the point where you enjoy listening to yourself. I believe this is very important: not only can you feel the music being played on the keyboard, you can hear that it sounds good.

All of this brings us to an important aspect of playing an instrument: relaxation. The best musicians in any style of music are the ones who are relaxed. It is much easier to practice and to play if you are relaxed. Whatever you do to relax, whether it be meditation or physical exercise or yoga, try to do it, or some of it, before you play or practice. As you play/practice, be conscious of your shoulders, arms, wrists, and legs. They should not feel tight or tense. Like any other exercise you will have to get accustomed to the feeling of relaxation. When you are first learning a new activity you feel like closing in and hiding yourself; but be more brazen! Sit tall on the piano bench, take a deep breath and let your lungs and chest expand. Let the breath out slowly. You should feel better, and ready to take on new things!

CHOOSING A PIANO

Your choice of a piano can be a grand, an upright, or an electric keyboard

Your choice of instrument depends on several things: how much room you have; how much money you can spend; if the instrument will have to be moved often; and your preference. Remember that the piano is mechanical; the electric keyboard is electronic (even though some are made with weighted keys to imitate the action of a piano). The piano sound reacts to your touch and the way you press the keys. The electric keyboard will play softer or louder according to your touch, but cannot respond otherwise. If the instrument has to be moved often, consider an electric keyboard. You will also need a stand you can adjust to a comfortable height. When playing the forearms should be parallel to the floor.

Grand Piano

- Strings are stretched parallel to floor; the shorter the string, the higher the sound.

- There are over seven octaves.

- Sizes, measured from front to back, range from baby (4½ to 5½ feet), to medium (5½ to 7½ feet), to concert (7½ to 9½ feet).

- For smaller pianos, thicker strings help make up for the sonic deficiencies of shorter strings.

Upright Piano

- Strings are stretched vertically, and still go from long (lower) to short (higher).

- The keyboard is the same size as the grand.

- Sizes, measured from the floor to the top of piano, range from spinet (36 to 39 inches) to console or studio (40 to 47 inches) to full size (48 to 60 inches).

- Again, a smaller piano will have shorter and thicker strings.

Electric keyboards come with 64, 76, or 88 keys. Some have built-in speakers; others will need a speaker or speakers to plug into. WIth an electric keyboard you can plug in earphones, and no one can hear you playing. A flat, square pedal may come with your keyboard. You can purchase a more realistic damper pedal that looks and feels like the damper pedal on a real piano.

The features of the electric keyboard are as varied as the number of keyboards you see! Study the choices carefully; list the features you need, and the features that are extras.

If purchasing an acoustic piano, consider that the longer the strings, the better sound you will have. The better the tone, the more you will want to play. Shop around and play as many pianos as you can. If you feel shy about playing in front of other people, take a more experienced player with you. But do play keys from each section of the keyboard to hear its sound and feel the action (the ease with which the keys are pressed).

Electric Piano

- This one is made to look like a real upright piano, with a solid back and sides.

- It is not portable, and the speakers are built in.

- Sounds vary by brand and may include two or more different piano sounds, a harpsichord sound, an organ sound, and a vibraphone sound.

- Choices of sounds differ with each brand. There are plugs for attaching earphones, and perhaps a midi (musical instrument digital interface) device.

Portable Electric Piano

- This keyboard is easily moved, but there needs to be a stand to hold it (usually an extra purchase).

- Many portables need outside speakers to plug into (usually an extra purchase).

- You can plug in earphones, a pedal, and a midi connection to a computer.

- You can have many percussion sounds, and in some cases percussion rhythms for certain types of music (rock, swing, tango, waltz, etc.).

MOVING AROUND THE KEYBOARD
To get the feel of the piano, start with the black keys

Sit in the middle of the piano bench, facing the middle of the keyboard. Touch the two black keys in front of you, then other two-black-key groups, going either direction. Play them with any fingers, separately or in clusters. Do the same with the three-black-key groups. You are playing to hear the sound these keys make, and to feel at ease with moving along the keyboard. There are no "mistakes" when you play. Everything is experimental. Leave yourself open to playing the black keys different ways: louder, softer, single keys, clusters of keys, higher keys (going to the right), lower keys (going to the left). Maybe you will play three or four keys and it will remind you of a tune you know. See if you can find the rest of the tune. The simplest tunes you might find are "Hot Cross Buns" and "Mary Had a Little Lamb."

Two Black Keys; C-D-E

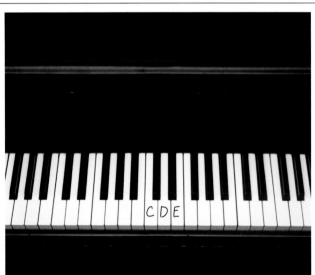

- Play the middle two black keys with any finger of the right hand; then play the three white keys that touch them: C-D-E.

- Sing names out loud as you play C-D-E up the keyboard (to the right).

- Hear each group get higher in pitch as you play higher.

- Start at the lower end (left) of the keyboard and, using the left hand, any finger, play C-D-E going higher (to the right).

Three Black Keys; F-G-A-B

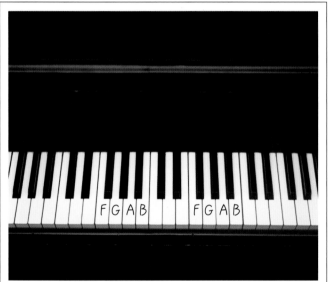

- Play a group of three black keys near the middle of the keyboard. Use any finger of the right hand; then play the four white keys that touch them: F-G-A-B.

- Sing names out loud as you play F-G-A-B up the keyboard (to the right).

- Hear each group get higher in pitch as you play higher.

- Start at the lower end (left) of the keyboard and, using the left hand, any finger, play F-G-A-B going higher (to the right).

All this playing is to make you comfortable at the keyboard. If you are relaxed, you will find it easier to play. Also, playing only the black keys makes a nice sound.

When you are accustomed to the black keys, and moving all over the keyboard, learn the names of the white keys that touch them. The first seven letters of the alphabet—A, B, C, D, E, F, G—are used to name the keys, and they are easily found if you associate them with the groups of black keys. As you practice playing these keys, try closing your eyes and feeling the two black keys, then playing either C, D, or E; play these in different places on the keyboard. Do the same with the three black keys: close your eyes, feel the three black keys, then play either F, G, A, or B.

Playing Position Check Points

- When playing, the forearms should be parallel to the floor, so bench height is important.

- Wrists need to be straight, not elevated, not pushed down.

- You should sit far enough away from the piano to allow arms to freely move along the keyboard.

- Place feet flat on the floor, about a foot apart.

More Tips for Playing Comfortably

- Sit on the front half of the bench; both hands should be able to play high (to the right) or low (to the left) on the keyboard.

- Use your kneecap (when sitting) to mold your hand into a relaxed position.

- When you play a key, the firm part of the finger is the tip and first joint. The rest of the hand and arm is relaxed.

PEDALS
The part of the piano that makes it special

There are usually three pedals: the right pedal is the sustaining pedal, also called the damper pedal. It controls the dampers (which keep the strings from vibrating). The left pedal is the soft pedal, also called the "una corda pedal" on a grand piano. The middle pedal can function in a variety of ways, depending on what type of piano you have.

It is useful to know how the key mechanism works. When you press a key, a felt hammer strikes three strings (or two, or one, as you go lower) that are tuned the same; the damper lifts off the strings, and the strings vibrate, creating the sound. An escapement action allows the hammer to bounce back so it does not inhibit the strings from vibrating. When you release the key, the damper goes onto the strings, stopping the vibrations and thereby the sound.

Pedals

- The right foot operates the right (damper) pedal.

- The left foot operates either the left or middle pedal.

- You can use the right and left feet at the same time.

Soft Pedal

- On a grand piano, the left, or soft pedal shifts the hammers slightly to the right so that they strike two strings instead of three.

- On an upright piano, the soft pedal moves the hammer rail closer to the strings so that the hammers do not have far to go to strike the strings.

With the ball of your right foot, press the right pedal, keeping the heel on the floor. All the dampers are lifted away from the strings; all the strings can vibrate. If you simply speak loudly and sharply, strings will vibrate in response. Still pressing the pedal, play one key. Notice the full, rich sound. Release the pedal and play the same note. The sound is much drier.

Now have some fun with your piano! Press the damper pedal with the right foot and play black keys only, but play them all over the keyboard. What a great sound! You sound like you've been taking lessons for years! Play some white keys. It is starting to sound murky, so release the pedal. This "having fun" should be a part of your practice routine. It helps you relax and allows you to look at your hands and fingers to see their playing shapes.

Using the Pedals

- The pedal is pressed down with the ball of the foot, while the heel remains on the floor.

- Pedal indications in music may be a solid line under notes to be pedaled, or the abbreviation, "Ped."

- Play black keys all over the keyboard with the damper pedal pressed, and listen to the full, sustained sound.

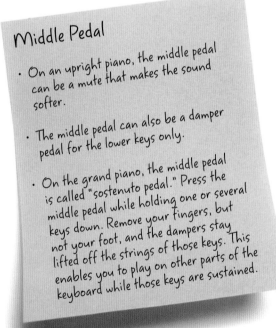

Middle Pedal

- On an upright piano, the middle pedal can be a mute that makes the sound softer.

- The middle pedal can also be a damper pedal for the lower keys only.

- On the grand piano, the middle pedal is called "sostenuto pedal." Press the middle pedal while holding one or several keys down. Remove your fingers, but not your foot, and the dampers stay lifted off the strings of those keys. This enables you to play on other parts of the keyboard while those keys are sustained.

FINGER PATTERNS & NUMBERS
Along with the note symbols, the finger numbers help you remember patterns

Music is read by patterns. Just as you read a book by joining several words in a glance, you read music by joining several notes and making sense of those notes. "Making sense" starts with intervals, or the distances of notes/keys from each other. Be sure you understand that "up" on the page means to the right on the keyboard. "Down" on the page means to the left

on the keyboard. You can get used to this direction-interval combination by first playing on the black keys down the keyboard, listening to the sound of "lower." Combine this with finger number practice, noting that as the right hand plays down, the finger numbers are backwards; i.e. fingers 4-3-2 playing down the three black keys. In the left hand, playing down the

Finger Numbers

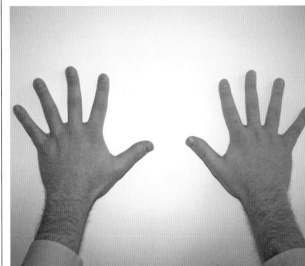

- The thumb, although not technically a finger, is the strongest digit; so it is no. 1.

- On the other side of the hand is the pinky; it is no. 5.

- The longest fingers are: index, 2, middle, 3, and ring, 4.

- An exercise: lay hands flat, palms down, on a table; tap fingers 3, then 4, then 5. End with tapping fingers 2, then 1.

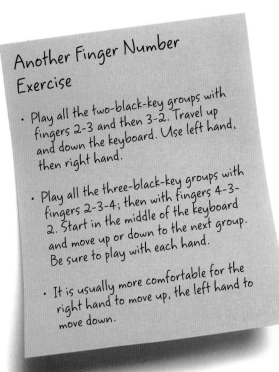

Another Finger Number Exercise

- Play all the two-black-key groups with fingers 2-3 and then 3-2. Travel up and down the keyboard. Use left hand, then right hand.

- Play all the three-black-key groups with fingers 2-3-4; then with fingers 4-3-2. Start in the middle of the keyboard and move up or down to the next group. Be sure to play with each hand.

- It is usually more comfortable for the right hand to move up, the left hand to move down.

keyboard indicates fingers 2-3-4 on the three black keys.

Now choose three white keys to play—G-A-B, for example—and let both hands play, one at a time, that particular set of white keys nearest each hand. Play down the keyboard and notice that as you play each note, the letter names of the keys are backwards; B-A-G. The right hand fingers are 4-3-2; the left hand fingers are 2-3-4.

Do the same for other groups of three white keys: D-E-F, for instance; or A-B-C. Always notice the direction—up for higher, down for lower.

Fingers on Consecutive White Keys (2nds)

- You can begin to feel finger/music patterns by practicing finger numbers on the white keys.

- Fingers 2-3, or 3-2, can play keys F-G. These are next-door-neighbor white keys, or 2nds.

- Play all the F-G's on the piano with fingers 2-3 (right hand), or fingers 3-2 (left hand).

- Practice playing fingers 2-3-4 (right hand) on F-G-A; fingers 4-3-2 (left hand) on F-G-A. Play all the notes of those names on the piano. Sing the names of the notes as you play.

Fingers Playing Skips (3rds)

- You can practice skipping white keys. When you skip a white key, skip a finger. This interval is called a 3rd.

- Play G up to the next B with right hand fingers 2 to 4. Listen for the pleasant sound (consonance) as you play back and forth, G-B-G-B.

- Play an F up to the next A with right hand fingers 1 to 3.

- Play all the above with the left hand, below the middle of the keyboard.

LISTENING

A very important and often neglected aspect of playing music is listening to music

These days there is background music everywhere we go: in the bank, the dentist's office, the restaurant. I suppose someone decided this background music was relaxing. But all it has done is teach us NOT to really listen to music.

A big part of playing an instrument is hearing. We can close our eyes and still play the piano, but if we close our ears, it is very difficult to play.

Take a few moments to listen to a different kind of music. If you only know popular music, try listening to a classical piece. If you prefer classical, try listening to some popular music. If you have never thought about what you are hearing, try these steps from my friend, Kathleen Adkins:

The Active Brain

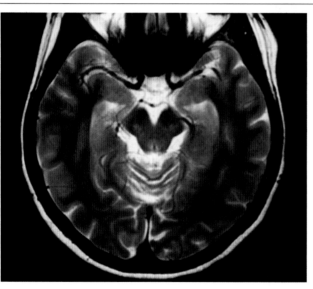

- Not only are your brain cells activated by playing an instrument, they actually "light up" when you actively listen to music.

- Brains trained to listen to music passively—at gas stations, in elevators—must be retrained to listen actively.

Listening While Playing

- Play the three black keys, as a cluster, then one note at a time.

- Listen with your eyes closed; play up (to the right), then down (to the left).

- Can you hear the difference between the up and down patterns?

- Look at your hands as you move the right hand up to the next group of three black keys and play them up, then down.

- Do the same with the left hand, but the next group of three black keys down.

Step 1. Listen to the music. Set aside enough time to listen to the whole piece without distractions. Sit quietly and focus only on listening. Don't let it become background music! Absorb it as completely and attentively as you can.

Step 2. Wait a few hours or a day and listen to the same piece again.

Once again, block out or eliminate distractions. This time, watch out for two things:

a. Familiar parts. Do you recognize melodies, passages, and harmonies from the first listening?

b. Your emotions. Does the music make you feel joyful? Sad? Let that feeling flow freely

Step 3. Listen to the same piece a third time. Do the same things you did in steps 1 and 2. Add one more thing: anticipation. See if you can anticipate a melody, an orchestral color, a harmony, before it happens. Do you find yourself looking forward to a phrase or chord? The more you listen to a great piece, the deeper your response to it will become.

Differences with the Pedal

- Press your right foot down on the far right pedal. Then play a note.

- Do you hear how the note resonates and lingers?

- Now lift the foot off the pedals and play the same note again. Do you hear the difference?

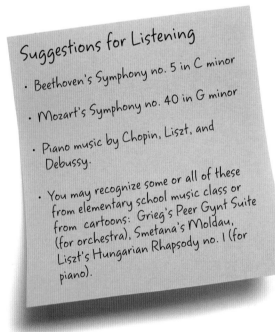

Suggestions for Listening

- Beethoven's Symphony no. 5 in C minor

- Mozart's Symphony no. 40 in G minor

- Piano music by Chopin, Liszt, and Debussy.

- You may recognize some or all of these from elementary school music class or from cartoons: Grieg's Peer Gynt Suite (for orchestra), Smetana's Moldau, Liszt's Hungarian Rhapsody no. 1 (for piano).

RHYTHM NOTATION
See how the rhythm is organized

Western music is organized into measures, separated by bar lines. At the beginning of the piece there is a time signature that tells you the number of beats in a measure (often called a "bar") and what kind of note gets one beat. Measures help you to see how the melody and the harmony are grouped. ("Melody" is the horizontal aspect of music; "harmony" is the vertical aspect.)

Let's use a familiar nursery rhyme, "Baa, Baa, Black Sheep."

Baa, baa, black sheep
Have you any wool?
Yes sir, yes sir,
Three bags full.

Reading the Music

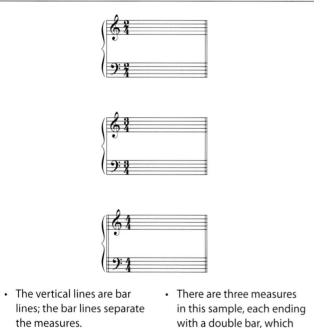

- The vertical lines are bar lines; the bar lines separate the measures.

- The time signature shows the number of beats in each measure, and the kind of note that equals one beat.

- There are three measures in this sample, each ending with a double bar, which should be used at the end of each piece of music.

Understanding Beats and Rhythm

- Use a pencil to circle the time signature.

- Review in your mind what each of these numbers mean.

- Set up a regular beat by counting two measures out loud.

- Tap the rhythm as you count out loud.

Each line of this poem can be one measure of a rhythmic pattern, each measure having four beats. The first line has four beats. The second line has words that are quoted twice as fast, until the word, "wool," which is held for two of the basic beats. Line three has four beats, and line four has two basic beats and "full" is twice as long, matching the word, "wool."

The time signature for this would be 4/4; the top or first number means there are four beats in each measure (in this case, line), and the bottom or second number means that a quarter note equals one.

So "basic" beats are quarter notes; this can change, but for now it is enough. A half note equals the time of two quarter notes. When notes are faster than the basic beat, they are usually twice as fast. These are called eighth notes. Two eighth notes fill the time of one quarter note. Sixteenth notes are twice as fast as eighth notes. Four sixteenth notes fill the time of one quarter note, or two sixteenth notes fill the time of one eighth note. It is getting complicated, so let's look at some samples.

Skip to My Lou

traditional

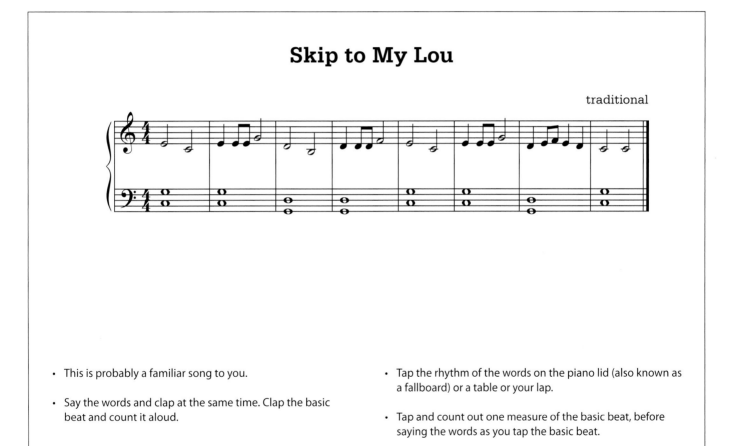

- This is probably a familiar song to you.

- Say the words and clap at the same time. Clap the basic beat and count it aloud.

- Tap the rhythm of the words on the piano lid (also known as a fallboard) or a table or your lap.

- Tap and count out one measure of the basic beat, before saying the words as you tap the basic beat.

RHYTHM & NOTE VALUES
Fascinating rhythm! Feel it; clap it; read it

If you tap or clap the rhythm of a familiar song, other people usually recognize it. So, knowing the rhythm of a piece of music goes a long way in learning and notating that music.

Try this exercise: walk at an easy pace; clap once for every step; count out loud, one number for each step—one, two, three, four. Think of a simple song or nursery rhyme, and say it in rhythm as you walk. If you prefer sitting, put both hands flat on a table or your lap and use your hands to "walk" (tap lightly) the regular beats or pulses. Notice, as you say the words to your regular beat, that some words are held longer than others, and that you can tap two steps to one word. Since the quarter note is the basic beat, each step can equal a quarter note.

Table of Note Values and a Pattern to Clap

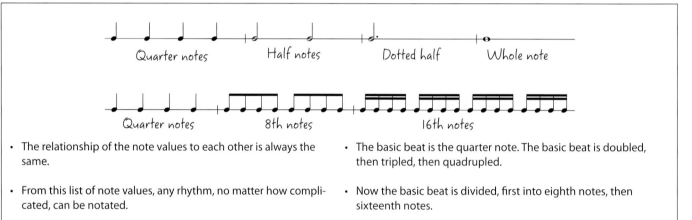

- The relationship of the note values to each other is always the same.

- From this list of note values, any rhythm, no matter how complicated, can be notated.

- The basic beat is the quarter note. The basic beat is doubled, then tripled, then quadrupled.

- Now the basic beat is divided, first into eighth notes, then sixteenth notes.

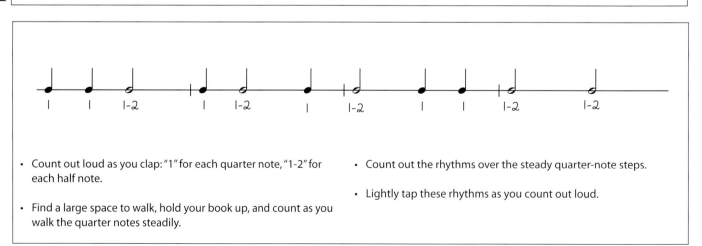

- Count out loud as you clap: "1" for each quarter note, "1-2" for each half note.

- Find a large space to walk, hold your book up, and count as you walk the quarter notes steadily.

- Count out the rhythms over the steady quarter-note steps.

- Lightly tap these rhythms as you count out loud.

12

We use measures to organize the patterns into a regular number of beats—two, three, four, five, six, and sometimes more. In the time signature the top number informs you of the number of beats in a measure. The bottom number is a symbol of the kind of note that equals one beat. In these beginning instructions we will use the number 4 (a symbol for quarter note) as the bottom number, although it is possible to use any note value to equal one beat.

ZOOM

Yes, there are 32nd and 64th notes; to notate these, add a flag or a beam to the note(s). If a 16th note has two beams or flags, the 32nd note will have three beams or flags; the 64th note will have four beams or flags. You can find examples in slow movements (usually the second movement) of classical sonatas by Haydn, Mozart, and Beethoven.

MUSIC NOTATION

Rhythm Patterns to Clap or Tap

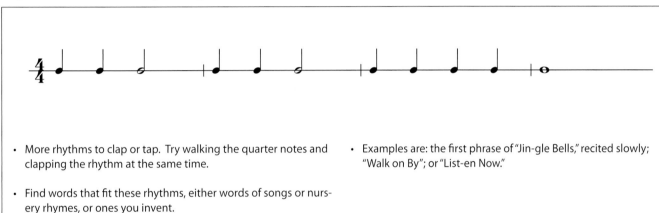

- More rhythms to clap or tap. Try walking the quarter notes and clapping the rhythm at the same time.

- Find words that fit these rhythms, either words of songs or nursery rhymes, or ones you invent.

- Examples are: the first phrase of "Jin-gle Bells," recited slowly; "Walk on By"; or "List-en Now."

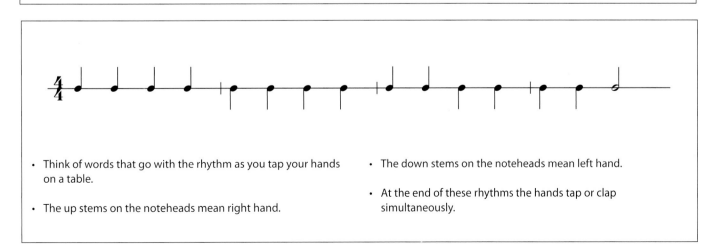

- Think of words that go with the rhythm as you tap your hands on a table.

- The up stems on the noteheads mean right hand.

- The down stems on the noteheads mean left hand.

- At the end of these rhythms the hands tap or clap simultaneously.

MORE RHYTHM
You are surrounded by the "beat," or the pulse of life

In Western music, rhythm has been traditionally organized into measures, with a set number of beats per measure. We call this organization "meter."

The first beat of the measure is called the downbeat, and is usually the strongest beat in the measure. A waltz has three beats per measure and is felt as ONE, two, three; ONE, two, three. The march rhythm usually has two or four beats per measure; it is felt as ONE, two, ONE, two, or as ONE, two, three, four, ONE, two, three, four.

Think of "Hot Cross Buns," or "Twinkle, Twinkle Little Star," or "Mary Had a Little Lamb," when you count two or four. "My Darling Clementine" has three beats in a measure. Take a

Hot Cross Buns

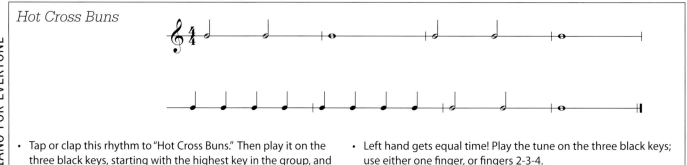

- Tap or clap this rhythm to "Hot Cross Buns." Then play it on the three black keys, starting with the highest key in the group, and using one finger, or fingers 4-3-2.
- Now play the tune on B-A-G. Use one finger, or fingers 4-3-2.

- Left hand gets equal time! Play the tune on the three black keys; use either one finger, or fingers 2-3-4.
- Left hand plays the tune on B-A-G, fingers 2-3-4.

London Bridge

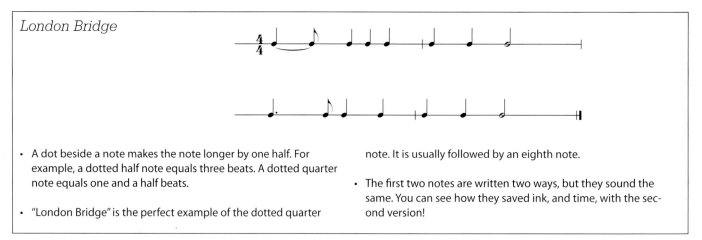

- A dot beside a note makes the note longer by one half. For example, a dotted half note equals three beats. A dotted quarter note equals one and a half beats.
- "London Bridge" is the perfect example of the dotted quarter

note. It is usually followed by an eighth note.

- The first two notes are written two ways, but they sound the same. You can see how they saved ink, and time, with the second version!

moment to think of these songs: sing them, or say the words in rhythm. Can you feel where the beat is stronger? The strongest beat is not always the first note of the song. The strongest beat in "Clementine" occurs on the first syllable of the word, "DAR-ling."

The two numbers at the beginning of each piece of music make up the time signature. The top number tells you how many beats are in a measure. The bottom number tells you what kind of note equals one beat. These are not fractions!

MUSIC NOTATION

Ode to Joy

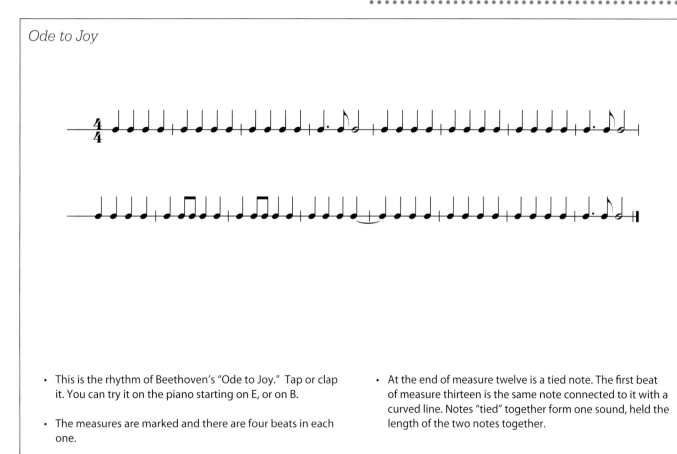

- This is the rhythm of Beethoven's "Ode to Joy." Tap or clap it. You can try it on the piano starting on E, or on B.

- The measures are marked and there are four beats in each one.

- At the end of measure twelve is a tied note. The first beat of measure thirteen is the same note connected to it with a curved line. Notes "tied" together form one sound, held the length of the two notes together.

THE ORIGINS OF NOTATION
The history of music notation flows logically from dots over the words

First, words of a religious chant were written on a page; the tune for the words was passed from one generation of choir members to another, until someone got a bright idea to put dots over the words to remind the singer of the movement of the tune. If the dots went higher, the tune went higher. If the dots went lower, the tune moved downward.

The next step in this simplified history of notation was one line drawn above the words to represent one definite pitch (the highness or lowness of a sound). The definite pitch letter (A, B, C, D, E, F or G) was written at the beginning of the line. If the tune went up from the lined note, the dots went above the line. If the tune moved downward from the lined note, the dots went below the line.

With the addition of other lines, the dots became line notes

Medieval Chant Notation

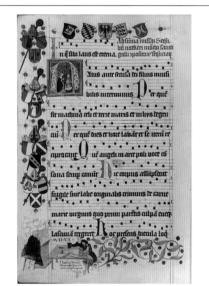

- The symbols over the words are called "neumes," from the Greek "neuma," which means sign or nod. Notice that they rise and fall, following the contour of the melody.

- The neumes were reminders of the chant. The singer would have memorized the exact melody.

- The conductor of the choir would indicate with his hand the rise and fall of the melody.

"Oh! Susanna," Verse

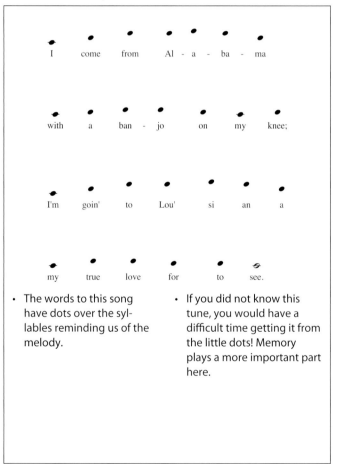

- The words to this song have dots over the syllables reminding us of the melody.

- If you did not know this tune, you would have a difficult time getting it from the little dots! Memory plays a more important part here.

and space notes. If you played or sang A up to B, it looked like a space note up to the next line, or a line note up to the next space.

As you sit at the keyboard with the book open, visualize the direction of the dots over the words and connect it with the appropriate direction on the keyboard.

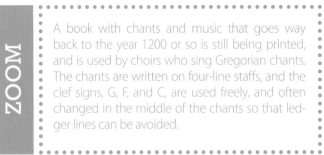

ZOOM

A book with chants and music that goes way back to the year 1200 or so is still being printed, and is used by choirs who sing Gregorian chants. The chants are written on four-line staffs, and the clef signs, G, F, and C, are used freely, and often changed in the middle of the chants so that ledger lines can be avoided.

MUSIC NOTATION

Medieval Chant Notation

- Notice the one line above the Latin words, with the letter "F" at the beginning.

- The other markings were indications for how long to hold notes and how to sing them.

"Oh! Susanna," Verse

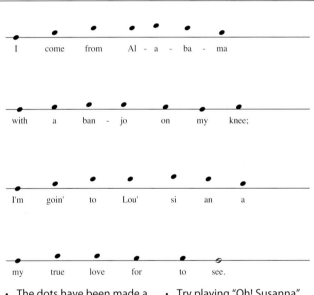

- The dots have been made a little more specific by adding a line above the words, indicating the first note of the line.

- Try playing "Oh! Susanna" on the piano, starting on middle C.

- The first three keys are intervals of a 2nd part: C, up a 2nd D, up a 2nd E.

17

TREBLE & BASS CLEFS
A place for all the high notes and low notes on the staff

By the year 1400, notation had developed into a staff with five lines and four spaces: high notes, or treble notes, are indicated on the treble staff; low notes, or bass notes, are indicated on the bass staff. ("Bass" is pronounced like "base.")

There are line notes and space notes. Notice the first two photos below, showing treble G down to middle C on the

Treble Staff, then treble G down to middle C on the keyboard. There is no line for middle C, so an extra line (ledger line) has to be drawn through the note.

Photos three and four show bass F up to middle C on the bass staff, then bass F up to middle C on the keyboard. Again, there is no line for middle C, so an extra line has to be drawn

Treble Staff

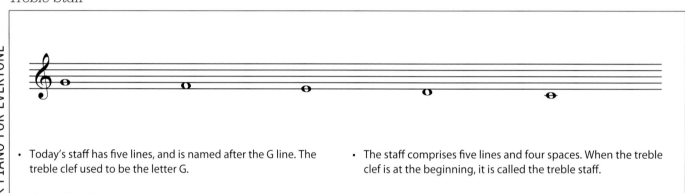

- Today's staff has five lines, and is named after the G line. The treble clef used to be the letter G.

- The treble ("high") clef is also called "G clef," and indicates the second line from the bottom as G above middle C.

- The staff comprises five lines and four spaces. When the treble clef is at the beginning, it is called the treble staff.

- Using the marker note, treble G, the keys from G down to middle C are written Line-Space-Line-Space-Line.

Treble G and Middle C on Keyboard

- When seated facing the middle of the keyboard, the C nearest the middle is called middle C.

- Treble G (the "marker" note) is the first G above middle C.

- Notes written on the treble staff are for women's

voices, higher (tenor) men's voices, violins, flutes, etc., and the high keys (around and above middle C) on the piano.

- Play all the white keys from treble G down to middle C with the right hand. Use one finger; then use fingers 5-4-3-2-1.

through the note.

Usually the treble clef sign is used for the top staff (right hand), the bass clef sign is used for the bottom staff (left hand). But there are times when both hands play above middle C on the piano; then the treble clef sign is used on both staffs. Conversely, there are times when both hands play below middle C; then the bass clef sign is used on both staffs.

Bass Staff

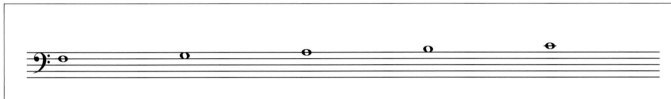

- The bass ("low") clef, is also called the "F clef," and indicates the 2nd line from the top as the first F below middle C. The F clef used to be the letter F.

- When the bass clef is at the beginning of the staff, it is called the bass staff.

- Using the marker note, bass F, the keys going up to middle C are line-space-line-space-line. They are all next-door-neighbor notes.

Bass F and Middle C on the Keyboard

- When seated facing the middle of the keyboard, the C nearest the middle is called middle C.

- Bass F (the "marker" note) is the first F below middle C.

- Notes written on the bass staff are for men's bass and baritone voices, cel-los, trombones, etc., and the low keys (around and below middle C) on the piano.

- Play all the keys from bass F up to middle C with the left hand. Use one finger; then use fingers 5-4-3-2-1.

THE GRAND STAFF
Twenty-two places for notes; 88 keys on the piano?!

When you bracket the bass and treble staff together, you have a grand staff—the upper staff is for right hand notes, the lower staff is for left hand notes. This gives you a good range of 22 white keys. But what if you want to notate and play below or above this range?

You could draw another line all the way across the staff to locate more notes. But that would make it difficult to read. In A.D. 1300 the staff for the church chants consisted of four lines. The clef signs used would change if the chant went too high or too low. But in modern times we recognize the value of the ledger line, a small segment of the extra line, just big enough to fit over, under, or through the note. Ledger line

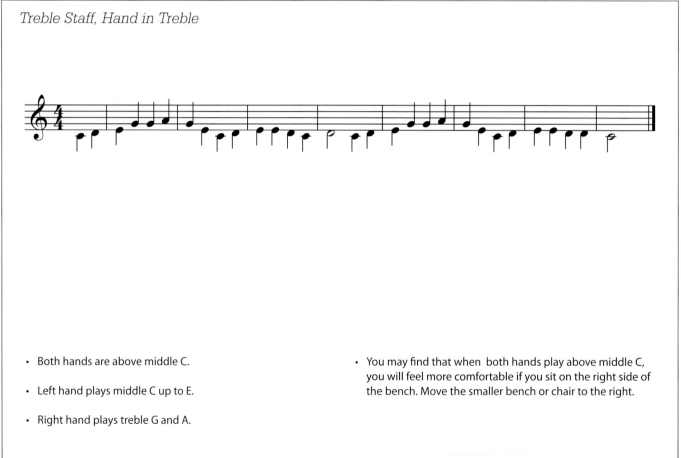

Treble Staff, Hand in Treble

- Both hands are above middle C.

- Left hand plays middle C up to E.

- Right hand plays treble G and A.

- You may find that when both hands play above middle C, you will feel more comfortable if you sit on the right side of the bench. Move the smaller bench or chair to the right.

KNACK PIANO FOR EVERYONE

notes are extensions to the staff.

When a melody is written on one staff, but played by both hands, the note stems indicate which hand is to play which notes: up-stem notes (stems drawn on the right side of the notehead) are for the right hand; down-stem notes (stems drawn on the left side of the notehead) are for the left hand.

Below, see two ways to notate "Oh! Susanna." The first one shows the melody on the treble staff. The second one shows the melody on the grand staff. When there is only one hand

playing from one staff, the notation guidelines indicate that on notes below the middle line, stems go up (on the right side of the note). On the middle line and higher, the stems of the notes go down (on the left side of the note).

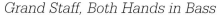

Grand Staff, Both Hands in Bass

- Both hands are above middle C.

- Right hand plays treble G and A.

- Left hand plays from middle C up to E.

- Again, you will feel more comfortable playing both hands above middle C, if you move to the right side of the bench; or if you move your smaller bench or chair to the right.

"OH! SUSANNA" IN NOTATION
A look at our "theme" melody on the staff

I have selected one familiar Stephen Foster song to illustrate each new aspect of notation. You can see, at this point in your piano education, how "Oh! Susanna" looks on a single staff with both hands playing, and on the grand staff with both hands playing.

Let's take a moment to plan the learning of this piece. Your left hand will only play three notes when they occur in the piece—C, D, E. Use the three longest fingers for this—4-3-2— and you see that I have marked those finger numbers under the notes, C, D, E. If you don't feel comfortable playing with the left hand, finger 4 should play middle C slowly and deeply five times. Do the same for finger 3 on D and finger 2

Treble Staff Melody, Both Hands

Oh! Susanna

Stephen Foster

- The down-stem notes are played with the left hand.

- The up-stem notes are played with the right hand.

- Can you name the first note in each hand?

- Notice the finger numbers over the notes. This will help you learn the pattern of intervals more easily. Writing the names over the notes does not help with the learning of the pattern.

22

on E. Remember to keep the hand, wrist, and arm relaxed.

Now play fingers 4-3-2 in a row, just as it is marked in the music, but play slowly and repeat five times.

The right hand will play treble G with finger 3, and the A above it with finger 4. Practice those two fingers the way you practiced the left hand keys. The finger pattern in the music is 3,3,4,3, so play that pattern slowly five times. Keep the hand, wrist and arm relaxed.

Play "Oh! Susanna" slowly; it won't sound the way you want

it to, but you need to have control over the fingers, and slow playing does the trick!

This is only the verse of the song; later on you will learn the chorus, or refrain. Do you know what the difference is? In the verse, the tune is the same but the words change each time. In the refrain, the words and tune are the same each time.

Grand Staff Melody

Oh! Susanna

Stephen Foster

- "Oh! Susanna" is played on the same place on the keyboard.

- The left hand notes are on the bass staff; right hand notes are on the treble staff.

- The song is played exactly as before.

- Again, the finger numbers are written over or under the notes. You must learn the names of notes, but seeing the finger pattern is more helpful in learning a piece.

RHYTHMS OF FAMOUS TUNES
Melodies you can clap or tap easily, because they are famous!

Be aware of the rhythmic pattern of whatever piece you are playing, or singing, or clapping. If you establish the rhythmic patterns first, before learning the notes or fingering, it helps you learn new music much faster.

When you are able to clap the rhythms of famous tunes or verses, and feel free with the beat, you will make music with much more ease and freedom. When you know what

the familiar rhythms look like, you will be able to transfer the feel and the knowledge of the rhythmic patterns to your new pieces.

Counting out loud helps the brain to grasp the rhythmic patterns. If you don't have a private space in which to work, and there are people around you, you may feel embarrassed to count out loud; but let this be a stimulus to make a private

Can You Name the Tunes?

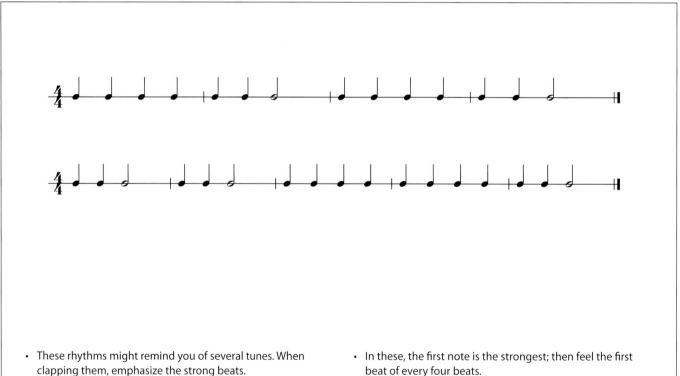

- These rhythms might remind you of several tunes. When clapping them, emphasize the strong beats.

- In these, the first note is the strongest; then feel the first beat of every four beats.

space and private time for yourself.

You can play a game with your family members and/or friends. One person claps the rhythm of a well-known tune and other people guess what the tune is. It is amazing that only the rhythm can make a tune recognizable!

Below are some rhythm patterns that you can clap or tap, and then you can ask others to "name that tune."

ZOOM

Think about all the rhythmic illustrations around you: old movies, with Fred Astaire dancing to music or to drums only, or to the machine noises in the belly of a ship; a jazz drummer doing myriad improvisations without any other instruments but feeling a beat behind it all; construction noises that have a rhythm that the workers are not aware of; the windshield wipers in your car!

Mystery Tunes

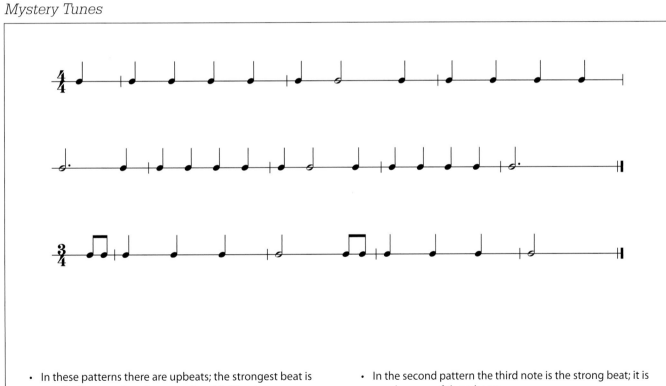

MORE BASICS

- In these patterns there are upbeats; the strongest beat is not the first one, but the second or third beat.

- In the first pattern, the second note is the strong one. Using the strong beat as beat one, clap out four beats.

- In the second pattern the third note is the strong beat; it is number one of three beats.

MARKER NOTES & INTERVALS

It's quicker to read/play notation on the piano if you have marker notes

Marker notes are easy to see on the page, easy to see on the keyboard. There is symmetry to the picture of the grand staff with marker notes: both the treble G and bass F are line notes; the middle C's on both staffs look exactly the same but in opposite places.

You can practice finding and naming the notes/keys around the marker notes. Buy staff paper, or download it, and copy the grand staff (below left). Draw each of the marker notes; then draw the notes a 2nd above and below the marker notes. Practice saying and playing these notes.

It might be helpful to have a good-sized chart with the letters A, B, C, D, E, F, G written on it. Place it on your music stand

Grand Staff with Marker Notes

2nds and 3rds on the Keyboard

- See the symmetry of the marker notes on the staff?

- A picture is worth a thousand words, and it is very true here.

- Practice naming all the lines and spaces on the grand staff. Go up from each marker note (forward in the alphabet), then down from each marker note (backward in the alphabet). Name the notes going down the staff two or three times.

- When you are finding intervals, always think of the letter names of keys.

- For a 2nd, think letter names next to each other: C up a 2nd D, or C down a 2nd B.

- For a 3rd, skip one white key (one skipped key, plus two played keys, equals three): G up a 3rd B, G down a 3rd E.

so you can see the neighboring keys and notes around the marker notes. Play and say the notes out loud; for example, "G, up a 2nd, A"; or "G, down a 2nd, F." Use neighboring fingers, 2-3, or 3-4, or 1-2, to play these.

Now do the same for intervals of a 3rd. Instead of a chart, you can cut these letters into separate squares; take out the letter between a marker note and the 3rd above it or below it. Keep these "flash letters." They may come in handy.

GREEN ● LIGHT

Another helpful way to learn intervals is to sing the notes you just wrote, a 2nd above and below the marker notes, a 3rd above and below the marker notes. Sing the names of the notes so that you are establishing the sound of the intervals and reinforcing the note names in your mind.

2nds and 3rds in Our Melody

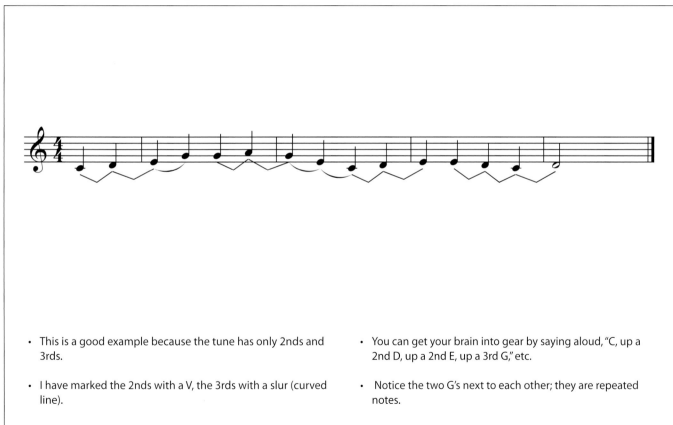

- This is a good example because the tune has only 2nds and 3rds.

- I have marked the 2nds with a V, the 3rds with a slur (curved line).

- You can get your brain into gear by saying aloud, "C, up a 2nd D, up a 2nd E, up a 3rd G," etc.

- Notice the two G's next to each other; they are repeated notes.

INTERVALS AROUND MARKER NOTES
Start relating sounds that you are familiar with to intervals you can play

I have a list of tunes both classical and popular that illustrate the intervals by their first two notes. A tune that starts with an octave (or an 8th) is "Over the Rainbow." "The Wedding March" (which is from an opera by Wagner) begins with a 4th. Think of tunes you know and try to discover the first two notes: are they close together? Are they far apart?

How close? How far? If you have recordings you can easily listen to, try to find the first two notes of your favorite piece(s). "Yesterday," the Beatles' song, begins with a 2nd. Schubert's Unfinished Symphony (the main theme) begins with a 4th going down, then a 4th up. A prominent musical theme in "2001 Space Odyssey" is actually the opening

4ths and 5ths on the Staff

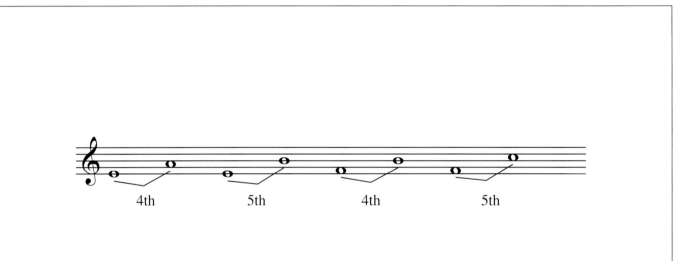

4th   5th   4th   5th

- The interval of a 4th goes line note to space note on the staff, or space note to line note.

- The interval of a 5th goes line note to line note, or space note to space note. A very distinctive look!

- Helpful hint: even-numbered intervals—2nds, 4ths, 6ths, 8ths—always appear line note to space note, or space note to line note.

- Odd-numbered intervals—3rds, 5ths, 7ths—always appear line note to line note, or space note to space note.

of "Thus Spake Zarathustra" by Richard Strauss. It begins by going up a 5th, then up a 4th.

As you look at 4ths and 5ths on the staff, think of "Here Comes the Bride" (the 4th) and "Twinkle, Twinkle Little Star," (the 5th) and associate the sound with the look of the interval on the staff, and with the feel of the interval on the keyboard. Try playing the interval with two hands, as in the photos, then with one hand. The 5th is played with fingers 1 and 5, the 4th is played with either fingers 1 and 4, or fingers 2 and 5. Play them blocked (both keys simultaneously) and

broken (one note at a time). Be sure to have both hands try these—equal time!

Also, you need to go in both directions—up and down—in identifying intervals. The popular song, "Feelings," goes down a 5th for the first two notes.

4ths on the Keyboard

- Play two keys, with two keys in between.

- Try playing the 4th with one hand, fingers 2 and 5, then 1 and 4.

- Equal time for the other hand!

- As you play 4ths in different places on the keyboard, listen for a different kind of 4th between F and B. Can you discover why this 4th sounds different from the 4th, G up to C?

5ths on the Keyboard

- The look of a 5th: Play two white keys, with three white keys in between.

- When playing a 5th with one hand, use fingers 1 and 5. Be sure the thumb slants slightly toward the wrist, and the pinky stands tall (even if it doesn't want to).

- As with the 4th, notice the different sound when you play from B up to F. It is still a 5th but it has a very different sound.

FINGERING RELATES TO INTERVALS
Basic hand position helps your muscles remember how to play certain intervals

Professional pianists hardly ever have to look at the keyboard. Their hands feel the keys and the intervals in the music.

You have already "felt" 2nds by using neighboring fingers. You have felt a 3rd with fingers 2 and 4 and 4ths and 5ths with each hand. Now practice using alternate fingers 1 and 3 on the 3rd. You can also play the 3rd with fingers 3 and 5, but

this will be difficult until the 5th finger is stronger. Play back and forth between finger 3 and finger 5, keeping a relaxed hand and wrist.

Play the interval of a 3rd with fingers 1 and 3, then 2 and 4, then 3 and 5.

Now work on various finger combinations for the 2nd.

Interval of a 3rd

- Notice the gentle slant of the thumb toward the wrist.

- Only the side of the tip of the thumb touches the key.

- The palm of the hand is high so that the fingers curve naturally.

- Play a 3rd from D to F with fingers 1-3. Play it again with fingers 2 and 4. Play again with fingers 3 and 5.

Interval of a 4th

- Notice the tip of finger 5 on the key. This helps the pinky stand "tall."

- Play finger 5 gently and softly, holding down the key for two counts. Do this seven times.

- When you play the fingers one at a time, rock the hand (almost imperceptibly) back and forth toward each playing finger.

Fingers 1 to 2 will be easy to play, but you must curve the second finger to keep it on its tip. Slant the thumb toward the wrist (that is, UP) so that only the side of the tip touches the key. Now play fingers 1-2, 1-2 several times.

Play fingers 2-3 several times, gently, and keep the thumb on its key, even though it is not playing.

When you play from finger 3 to finger 4, think of rocking your hand when each finger plays. In this way the arm and hand help the articulation of each finger, allowing the key of finger 3 to rise as the key of finger 4 goes down.

·············· GREEN ● LIGHT ··············

When practicing intervals in one hand, play them melodically (one note at a time) first. Play them back and forth until it feels easy. Then try them blocked, or harmonically (notes played simultaneously). Keep the wrist relaxed. Always practice the same in the other hand!

Interval Piece

M.A. Martin

A Bit of Itsy-Bitsy Spider

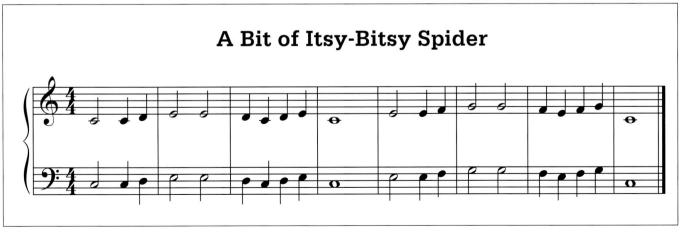

MORE BASICS

SYMBOLS FOR SILENCE
The beat goes on, even if the saxophone takes a break

If there are symbols for sound, then, conversely, there are symbols for silence. Music needs to breathe and these symbols are one way to accomplish this feat. Also, in ensemble music, whether it be string quartet, orchestra, or band, certain instruments are silent while others come to the forefront. For every kind of note, except dotted notes, there is a "rest."

Following the table of rests, I have put some rhythmic patterns to clap. The most efficient way to feel a rest is to use an action other than clapping. As you clap or tap, have your arm(s) move the opposite way for the rests. When you count out loud for the notes, whisper the count for the rests.

When you play music on the piano, you simply let the key up during the rest, so there is no sound. It is a small action but a necessary one to create the silence that is needed.

Table of Rests

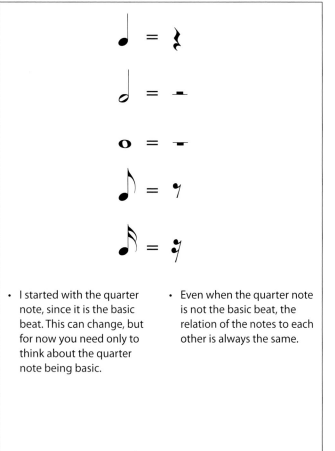

- I started with the quarter note, since it is the basic beat. This can change, but for now you need only to think about the quarter note being basic.

- Even when the quarter note is not the basic beat, the relation of the notes to each other is always the same.

Rhythms to Clap or Tap

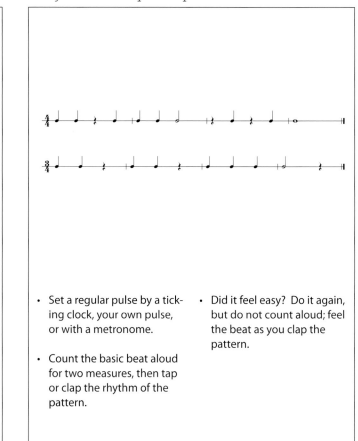

- Set a regular pulse by a ticking clock, your own pulse, or with a metronome.

- Count the basic beat aloud for two measures, then tap or clap the rhythm of the pattern.

- Did it feel easy? Do it again, but do not count aloud; feel the beat as you clap the pattern.

If you are tapping a rhythmic pattern, be sure to hold the hand down for a long note—half note or longer—as you count. When there is a rest, bring the hand up for the count. It is an action, but a silent one.

MORE BASICS

Rhythms to Clap or Tap

33

BASIC EXERCISES
Learning to play a piece of music requires a plan

To learn a skill, whether it be throwing a ball into a basket, serving a tennis ball, or playing music, requires some study, a plan of action, and drill, drill, drill.

A plan for learning a music piece: 1. Clap or tap the rhythm several times, until you have a sense of what it will sound like. 2. Look through the piece, name the first note in each hand, and plan the fingering for each note. 3. Play the piece slowly,

incorporating the rhythm pattern. Play it five more times.

Hopefully you are listening as you play. Ask yourself, "How did it sound?" "Did it sound the way I expected it to sound?" "Does it feel easy to play?" Then play the piece several more times.

The number of times you play a piece, or a section of a piece, depends on several things. Scientists who study the

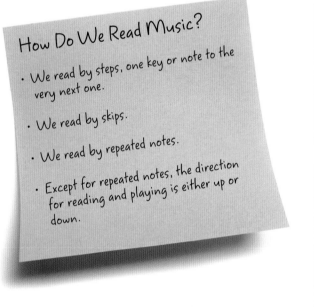

How Do We Read Music?

• We read by steps, one key or note to the very next one.

• We read by skips.

• We read by repeated notes.

• Except for repeated notes, the direction for reading and playing is either up or down.

Clapping the Rhythm of a Piece

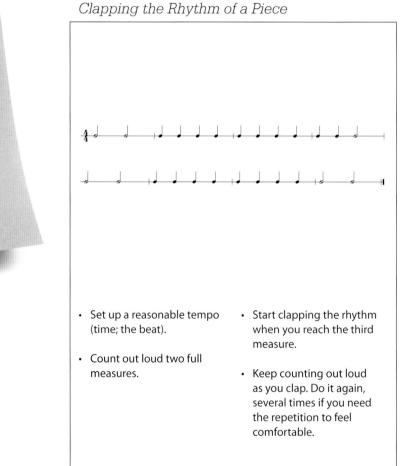

• Set up a reasonable tempo (time; the beat).

• Count out loud two full measures.

• Start clapping the rhythm when you reach the third measure.

• Keep counting out loud as you clap. Do it again, several times if you need the repetition to feel comfortable.

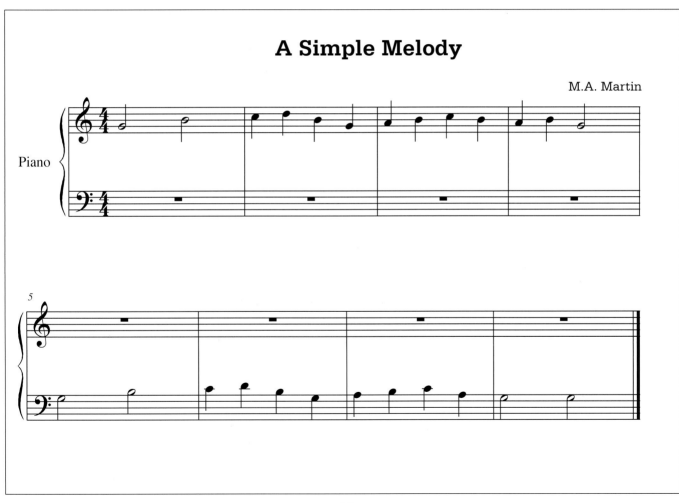

brain tell us that to really learn a pattern or skill (in this case one piece of music, or an exercise, or a part of a piece), you need to do it seven times correctly.

"Correctly" is the key word. Seven times with mistakes doesn't work. In playing music, you need to play slowly enough so that you can play it correctly.

GREEN ● LIGHT

There should be times when you simply play a piece to get through it, without stopping, in spite of mistakes. This may seem like a contradiction, but you need that side of the practice routine. If you are playing for a group of people singing for fun, you can't stop and fix a mistake.

A Simple Melody

M.A. Martin

Piano

LET'S PLAY!

TREBLE CLEF MELODIES
Women's voices, violins, flutes, trumpets, are just a few musical sounds that use treble clef

We read/play treble staff melodies for the higher sounds. Review the marker notes on the treble staff: treble G and middle C. Play each key and review 2nds above and below each marker, then 3rds above and below, 4ths and 5ths above and below.

You can use the "flash letters" that you made earlier. Put these on your music stand and remove letters for the 3rds, 4ths, and 5ths. You can quickly see the keys you should be playing and feeling, especially for the downward intervals.

When you play treble staff melodies, you can use one hand

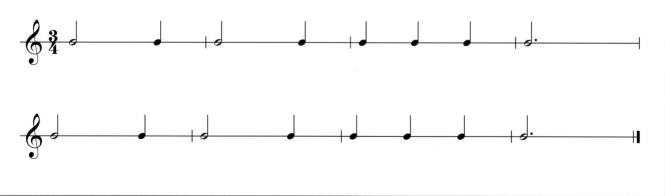

Treble Portion of Keyboard

- All the keys from middle C up are shown in this photo.

- On your piano keyboard, that includes all the keys to the right of middle C.

- Play keys from middle C up the keyboard, then play down. Listen to the quality of the high sounds.

- Listen to any kind of music, and pick out the instruments (or voices) that are performing the higher notes.

or both hands, depending on the range (lower to higher extremities) of notes.

You can look through the music to see if you will be able to play all the notes with one hand, without having to jump to another hand position. If you need two hands to play the melody, decide how many of the notes should be played with the left hand, how many in the right hand. Then decide which fingers will play which notes.

I know that all of this planning takes time; but each time you do it, it will take less time. A good music reader has to have the basic technique for music, plus the ability to decide immediately what technique is needed to play a particular passage of music. Your knowledge of intervallic patterns, plus the agility of your fingers to play independently and together, will certainly help you to become a good sight reader/player.

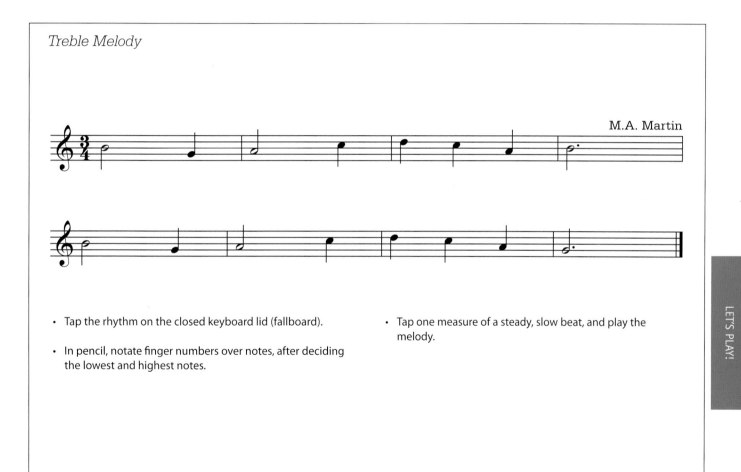

Treble Melody

M.A. Martin

- Tap the rhythm on the closed keyboard lid (fallboard).

- In pencil, notate finger numbers over notes, after deciding the lowest and highest notes.

- Tap one measure of a steady, slow beat, and play the melody.

BASS CLEF MELODIES

Men's voices, cellos, trombones, are a few musical sounds that use the bass clef

We read/play bass staff melodies for the lower sounds. Review the marker notes on the bass staff: bass F and middle C. Play each key and review 2nds above and below each marker, then 3rds above and below, 4ths and 5ths above and below.

Use the "flash letters" to find the names of the notes/keys quickly—F up a 3rd, A; F down a 3rd, D, for example. Saying the names aloud helps the mind to retain them.

If you have an electric keyboard with various instrument imitations, listen to them and decide if they use the lower range of notes, or the higher range, or both low and high sounds. Even the percussion selections have high and low qualities. A drum set has a great variety of sounds, from bass drum to

Bass Portion of Keyboard

- All the keys from middle C DOWN are shown.

- On your piano that includes all the keys to the left of middle C.

- Play the keys from middle C down the keyboard, then up to middle C. Listen to the quality of the low sounds.

- Listen to any kind of music and try to hear the lowest sounds and what instruments or voices perform them.

Keeping Your Piano in Tune

- If you have an acoustic piano, maintenance is important.

- Pianos need to be tuned once a year, preferably at the same time of the year.

- Humidity and temperature play an important role in the upkeep of your piano.

- Find out from your piano tuner how to best take care of your piano.

wood block to cymbal. Listen carefully as you become more sensitive to the higher, lower, and middle range sounds.

On your piano keyboard, you can really hear the difference between high and low if you learn a certain melody in the bass, then transfer it to the higher part of the keyboard. Now play the melody you learned for the treble part of the keyboard in the bass section of the keyboard. What a difference! Yet, it is the same tune.

ZOOM

The term, "bass," comes from Italian and French terms meaning "low." Why we pronounce it like the word, "base," I do not know. You have to remember how it is pronounced, and fortunately there are many instances in which you use the term, as in "bass violin," "bass clarinet," or "double bass."

Bass Melody

M.A. Martin

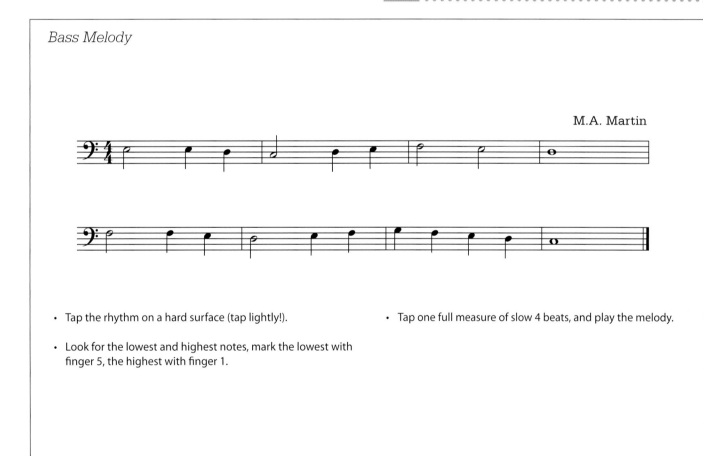

- Tap the rhythm on a hard surface (tap lightly!).

- Look for the lowest and highest notes, mark the lowest with finger 5, the highest with finger 1.

- Tap one full measure of slow 4 beats, and play the melody.

LET'S PLAY!

PIANO MELODIES
You need a staff for each hand, because the range of notes is very wide

The grand staff is the staff for keyboard music. The staff at the top is for the right hand; the staff at the bottom is for the left hand. The clef signs can change; sometimes music that is mostly above middle C will have both hands on the treble staff. Vice versa for the music that is mostly below middle C.

Below, there is one melody that is only melody; therefore the hands never play at the same time. But the sound goes from one hand to another without a break. This is called, "legato" (smooth and connected). Legato playing from one finger to another is rather like a see-saw effect: The finger

- This is a melody that goes from one hand to the other. Once you have learned to play it, try singing it, "la" for each note.
- When you sing, you have a true legato. Imitate that sound of connection with your fingers.

that plays one key does not lift (or let the key up) until the next one is down (you may have been playing this way naturally). You need to feel the same effect between hands; i.e., finger 2 of the left hand does not let the key up until finger 1 of the right hand is down. There should be no break in sound. Contrast this "touch" with a shorter sound for each note; let a little "light" in between notes. Then play the keys with a legato touch again. You can hear the difference in the sound of legato and non legato. Now play the keys even shorter, as if they were too hot to touch. This is a "staccato" touch.

Combine all these touches with your practicing. Play your own pattern of five different keys/fingers, starting on any key, and repeat it with a staccato touch, then legato touch, then non legato touch. If you are terrified you won't remember the pattern you just played, either write down the finger numbers, or play 1-2-3-4-5.

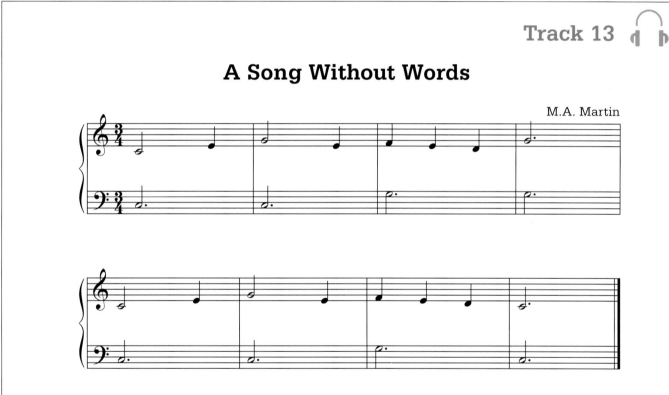

Track 13

A Song Without Words

M.A. Martin

- This piece has the melody in the treble staff, and an accompanying note in the bass staff. In other words, the hands play together.

- When hands first play simultaneously, a finger number over each pair of notes that play together helps enormously and keeps your eyes from looking back and forth at the music, then at the fingers.

LET'S PLAY!

MORE GRAND STAFF TUNES
How to get to Carnegie Hall? Practice, practice, practice

To enjoy playing the piano, and enjoy reading music as you play, you have to drill, practice, drill, practice. It is up to you how you do that, but it is important to relax and enjoy the process. It's good to have a goal—a large one, mixed with shorter-term goals—but you need to enjoy the journey to those goals.

Here are more melodies to "sight play." Always remember those practice steps—study the piece, practice the rhythm by tapping and counting out loud, mark in the fingering you need, name the first note in each hand, then play slowly. Keep going back in the book to play tunes you already know—they get easier and easier, and your fingers get stronger and stronger.

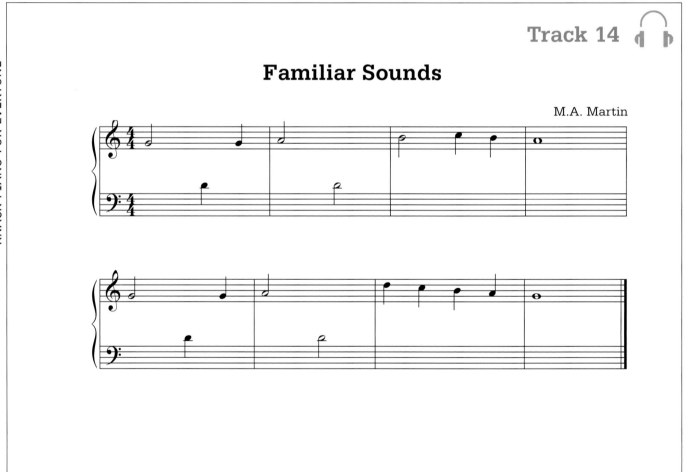

Track 14

Familiar Sounds

M.A. Martin

Purchase a piano book with tunes you can play right away. The only kind I discourage you from buying is a book with the names of notes *on* the notes. This will detract from seeing the music patterns.

If you already have, or wish to have a book with familiar tunes, and you only see music written for hands together, you can play the melody by itself.

Track 15

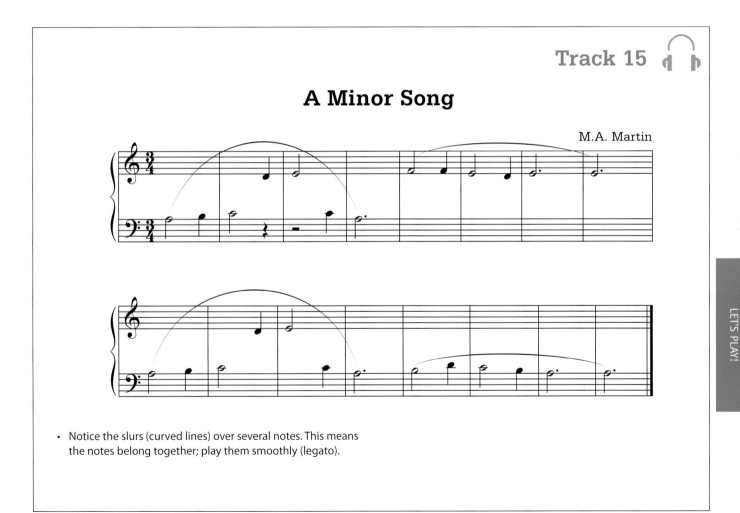

- Notice the slurs (curved lines) over several notes. This means the notes belong together; play them smoothly (legato).

THE OCTAVE SIGN
You need an easy way to get from here to there

Many years ago, composers and copyists discovered a way to avoid using lots of ledger lines when moving up or down to the same notes higher or lower. The interval of an eighth is also called an octave—cover eight keys and you will be at the same key higher or lower. Italian for octave is "ottava." When you want to play the same note or notes an octave higher, write an 8va sign over the passage, or one note, you wish to play higher. If it is several notes, draw a dotted line to encompass those notes.

If you wish to play the note or notes an octave lower, place the 8va sign below the notes, followed by a dotted line to include all the notes you want to play in that octave.

I suggested earlier that you play a melody that was written on the treble staff, in the bass staff, and vice versa. You can

How an Octave Looks

- It is easy to see the octave with the black keys.

- This is the interval of an 8th, which we call "octave" and for which the Italian word is "ottava."

- In music, the abbreviation 8va is used. If more than one note is up or down an octave, a dotted line encompasses those notes.

Octave Played with One Hand

- If your hand is large enough, or if you have a good stretch, you can play an octave with one hand.

- Physically, it is important to release the stretch immediately after you play the octave.

- The natural position for the hand is smaller than the octave, and you should return to that natural position after playing the octave.

notate that by putting an octave sign under or over the notes. Since you would want the complete piece to be moved, you don't have to put the dotted line. Just say, "Repeat 8va lower," or, "Repeat 8va higher."

This is a good time to practice a jump, or a leap to an octave above or below. If you play the piece where it is written, then repeat it an octave higher or lower. Lift from the relaxed wrists to move, but remember that the shortest line between two keys is a straight line, so don't make too big an arc.

Sometimes a piece will require you to move up or down two octaves. In that case, the sign, "15ma" is used. This stands for the Italian word for 15 notes, or a 15th.

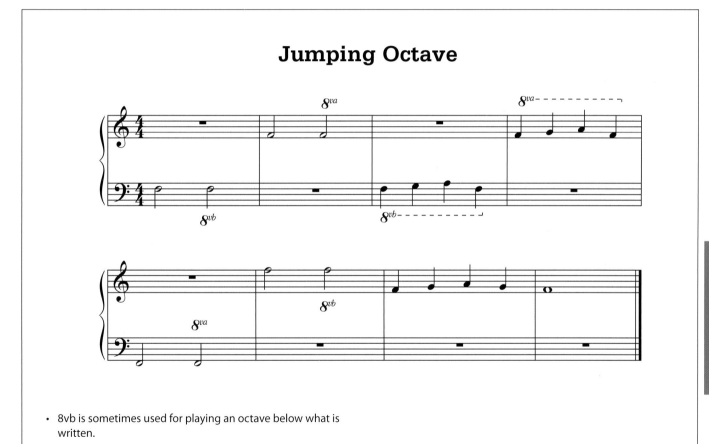

Jumping Octave

- 8vb is sometimes used for playing an octave below what is written.

BLACK KEY NAMES

At last, those important black keys are named

A sharp sign raises a key to the very next key, black or white. A flat sign lowers the key to the very next key, black or white. So, each black key has two names: G-sharp is the same key as A-flat.

Play every key, black and white, up the keyboard, one at a time. Listen to the sound of this chromatic scale. Name the keys aloud, F, F#, G, G#, etc. When you come to the gap where

there are no black keys, the very next white key has to take the name of the sharp; for example, B, B# (which is also C), E, E# (which is also F). So the C and F keys have two names.

Now go down the keyboard, playing a chromatic scale and naming the keys aloud, B, B♭, A, A♭, etc. When you come to the gaps where there are no black keys, the white key takes the name of the flat: F, F♭, C, C♭. Keys E and B are also flat keys.

Sharp Names of Keys

- There are two places on the keyboard in which the white keys are not separated by a black key.

- The note F is the same as E#; the note C is the same as B#.

- Have some fun playing these two white keys up and down the piano. Add some steady rhythmic interest.

Playing Sharp Keys

- Fingers 3 and 2 are as close as they can be on the keys.

- When you play a black and a white key, either together or one right after the other, the finger on the black key

should play it on the front edge of the key. The finger on the white key has to play close to the black key, and farther back on the key than usual.

46

This may seem confusing and illogical. It will only make sense when you study five-finger patterns and scales. Don't be concerned right now.

Listen for chromatic sounds in familiar tunes. The theme from *Jaws* begins with a very low, chromatic step.

When you draw a sharp sign in music, the central box of the sign is on the line or space of the note it is affecting. Likewise, the round or oval part of the flat sign should be on the line or space with the note.

In music, the sign for sharp or flat must come before the note (to the left of the note). When writing about sharps or flats, the sign comes after the note mentioned: for example, G♯.

Flat Names of Keys

- There are two places on the keyboard in which the white keys are not separated by a black key.

- The note E is the same as F♭; the note B is the same as C♭.

- Have some more fun playing these two white keys up and down the keyboard. Set a steady beat and play different rhythmic patterns. You are practicing rhythm, your fingers, and moving up and down octaves!

Playing Flat Keys

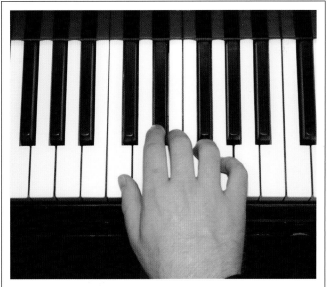

- Again, finger 3 and 2 are as close as they can be on the keys.

- Finger 2 is on the front edge of the black key. Finger 3 is close, and playing a little closer to the fallboard than usual.

- The fallboard is the part of the piano cabinet that covers the keys when they are not being played.

NATURALS
Naturals are signs for returning to the original note

Sharps, flats, and naturals are grouped under the heading "accidentals." Natural signs are often used in blues music. If you play the refrain of "St. Louis Blues" starting on E-flat, you have to follow it with E-natural, then C. The natural sign (♮) is needed here.

E♭ to E♮ in a C pattern, or F♮ to F♯ in a D pattern, usually in the left hand, is common in boogie-woogie style music.

Play the keys F, F♯, and F-natural. Say the names, or sing the names, as you play them. Do the same for C, C♯, and C♮. Play the same keys in the other hand so you are exercising both hands.

Now play some flat keys with their naturals: B, B♭, B♮. Sing the names as you play. Play A, A♭, A♮, singing or saying the names as you play.

Natural Sign on the Staff

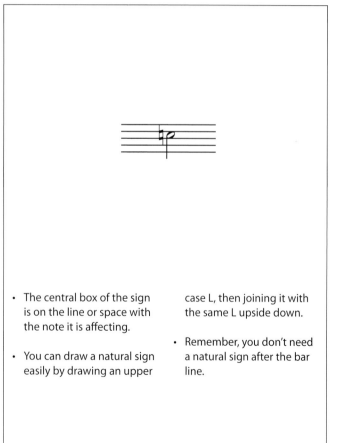

- The central box of the sign is on the line or space with the note it is affecting.

- You can draw a natural sign easily by drawing an upper

case L, then joining it with the same L upside down.

- Remember, you don't need a natural sign after the bar line.

The Natural Sign

- The bar line cancels the sharp or flat that has been added in a measure.

- In the same measure, to cancel a ♯ or ♭, a natural sign is used.

- A natural sign is not needed to show a sharp or flat that has been canceled after a bar line.

- The generic name of sharps, flats, and naturals, is "accidentals."

Even though musicians usually write sharp signs when ascending and flat signs when descending, have some fun playing a chromatic scale up by naming the keys C, D♭, D♮, E♭, E♮, all the way up one octave. Do the same scale down, naming the black keys sharps, followed by the ♮: C, B, A♯, A♮, G♯, G♮, etc., down to the next C.

ZOOM

A flat or sharp sign manipulates all the notes on the same line or space in the same measure. The bar line cancels the flat or sharp. To cancel the sharp or flat in the same measure, you need a natural sign in front of the note. A chromatic scale includes every key, black and white, in an octave. There are twelve different notes or keys in an octave.

Accidentally Accidentals

M.A. Martin

BLACK KEY NAMES

HALF STEPS & WHOLE STEPS
Two kinds of neighboring keys: get the feel of them

From one key to the very next key, black or white, is a half step. In other words, F to F♯ is a half step. You played lots of half steps when you learned sharps and flats.

There are two places (within an octave span) where half steps lie between two white keys: B to C and E to F. Otherwise, half steps are between black and white keys.

From one key to the next key, skipping one key, is a whole step (a whole step equals two half steps); in other words, F up to G, or E down to D.

Whole steps can occur between two white keys (G to A, for instance), two black keys (G♯ down to F♯), or between a black and white key (B up to C♯).

As you did with the black keys, feel the different combinations for half and whole steps by practicing each two

Half Step, White Key to Black Key

- Fingers 3 and 2 are very close.

- The sound of a half step when the two keys are played at the same time can be jarring.

- Play the half step with the left hand, very low on the keyboard.

- When one finger is on a black key, the next finger on a white key, play the black key on the front edge. The neighboring finger is very close to it, and away from the front edge of the white key.

Half Step, White Key to White Key

- This half step is a bit of a surprise, but the gap, where there is no black key, really helps you to feel your place on the keyboard.

- You played this when you studied sharps and flats, but get to know the names of the white keys where there are half steps: B to C, E to F.

- Play up and down on all these gaps. Set a steady beat and add rhythm to your playing.

successive fingers (1-2, 2-3, 3-4, 4-5) on half steps, then whole steps. Close you eyes to feel and hear the different sounds. Is there a tune you hear when you play a whole step up? "Are You Sleeping" is a good example. What about the half step? The theme from *Jaws* played low on the piano, is a half step.

Whole Step, White Key to White Key

- You must be aware of the black keys to know where you are playing.

- The first three notes of "Are You Sleeping" and "Oh! Susanna" are whole steps apart, going up.

- A whole step down gives you the start of "Yesterday."

- Play up on these white key whole steps F-G-A. Try playing one of the songs by ear.

- Play "Hot Cross Buns" or "Mary Had a Little Lamb" on these white key whole steps, A-G-F.

Whole Step, Black Key to Black Key

- You have been playing the three black keys from the beginning.

- When you play up the three black keys, can you hear, "Tennessee Waltz"?

- Play the songs you did on the white keys, on the three black keys. Listen, close your eyes, and play them.

- Now practice moving to the next lower group of three black keys. Now go higher. Play each hand to make your practice equal.

ENHARMONIC KEYS
Every key, black or white, has two names

There are two places on the keyboard that have no black key between the two white keys; those places are B to C and E to F. In order to sharp B, you must play C; C♭ is played on the B key. Likewise, E-sharp and F are the same key, F♭, and E are the same key.

These "gaps," where there are two white keys with no

black key in between, help you feel your way around the keyboard.

Play some exercises that have you jumping from gap to gap. Play fingers 2 and 3 on those two white keys that form a half step. Get ready with the right hand on one of the gaps, and the left hand on another gap. Set up a regular rhythmic

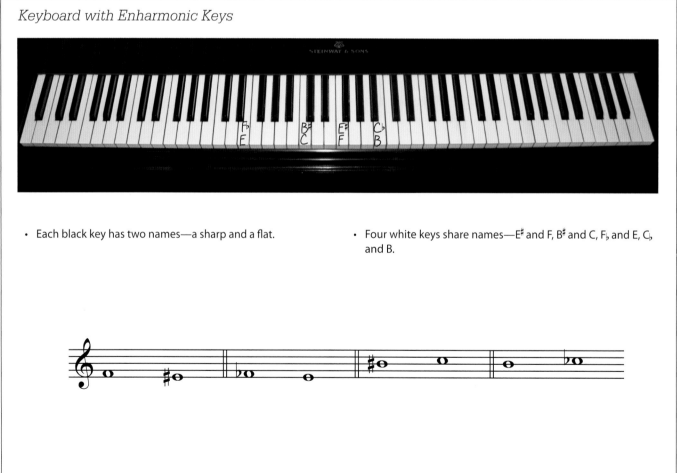

Keyboard with Enharmonic Keys

- Each black key has two names—a sharp and a flat.

- Four white keys share names—E♯ and F, B♯ and C, F♭, and E, C♭, and B.

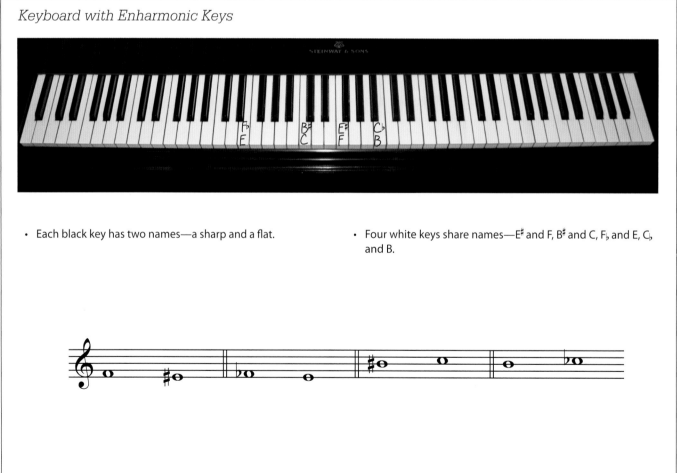

count and jump back and forth on different sets of white-key half steps. It is easiest if one hand at a time does the jumping, but when that feels comfortable, try jumping both hands at the same time.

To practice for accuracy, jump quickly to the next gap, then wait one or two counts before you actually play it. Each time you do it, the wait gets shorter.

To practice naming these enharmonic keys, start on the note C, and play up the keyboard on D, E, F, and G. Start on C♯ and play up the keyboard on D♯, E♯, F♯, and G♯. Name the notes aloud as you play. Play the same keys, but name them D♭, E♭, F, G♭, and A♭.

Play the same game starting on F. Play up the keyboard on G, A, B♭, and C. Then start on F♯ and play up on G♯, A♯, B, and C♯. Next, play the same keys, calling them G♭, A♭, B♭, B, and D♭.

NEW MARKERS

Start to read the higher and lower notes on the staff

Two new markers will help you read the highest and lowest notes on the staff. First, play the octave (with two hands) from treble G to high G. Line up the "flash letters" on your music stand, and play the 2nds, 3rds, 4ths, and 5ths above and below high G. On a piece of staff paper, draw these notes, and play them from the music. Remember to name

the intervals and notes out loud: for example, "high G, up a 4th, C."

For extra practice, play the patterns you first played around middle C and treble G on this higher part of the keyboard. Use the right hand.

Now play the octave from bass F to low F, with two hands.

High Notes

- The high notes on the treble staff are named around the marker note, high G.

- Play the keys, and name the intervals and notes up and down from high G out loud: G, down a 2nd, F; down a 2nd, E♭; etc.

- Notice there is a new C, an octave above middle C. It is a space note.

Treble G and High G

- The two keys are an octave apart; treble G is a line note, and high G is a space note.

- They sound the same, only one sounds higher.

- Play the other Gs on the piano. Listen to the sound, which will be the same but higher or lower.

Line up the "flash letters" on your music stand and play the 2nds, 3rds, 4ths, and 5ths above and below low F. On a piece of staff paper, draw these notes and play them from the music. Remember to name the intervals and notes out loud: for example, "low F, down a 4th, C."

Use the left hand to play the patterns you first read around middle C and bass F on this new place on the keyboard.

You'll notice when you read the notes on staff paper that you will need ledger lines as you go a 2nd, 3rd, 4th, and 5th up from high G, and down from low F. Remember that the ledger lines are extensions of the staff and should be placed accordingly. You need to be able to recognize whether a note is a space note or a line note when it falls below or above the staff.

Low Notes

- The low notes on the bass staff are situated around the marker note, low F.

- Play the keys and name the intervals and notes around low F out loud: F, up a 2nd, G; up a 2nd, A; etc.

- There is another C, an octave below middle C. It is a space note.

Bass F and Low F

- The two keys are an octave apart; bass F is a line note and low F is a space note.

- They sound the same, only one sounds lower.

- Play the other Fs on the piano and listen to the different higher and lower pitches.

THE SYMMETRY OF THE Cs
All the Cs on the grand staff are mirror images of each other

If you can see the five Cs easily, you can have more markers to help you read music. As you see from the music staff below, middle Cs on the treble and bass staffs are mirror images. When you go up an octave, and down an octave, to the next Cs, they, too, are mirror images of each other. An octave above and below those Cs are the high and low Cs,

and they too are mirror images. The Cs are the only notes that do this.

Keep the right hand on middle C and practice playing the octave below with the left hand, then crossing the left hand over the right hand to play the C above middle C.

Now do the opposite, keeping the left hand on middle C

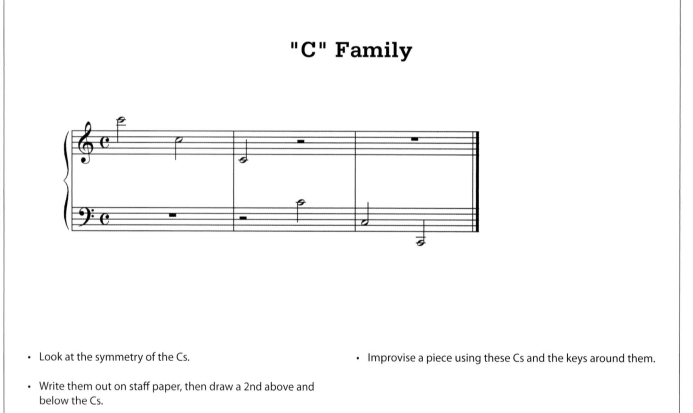

"C" Family

- Look at the symmetry of the Cs.

- Write them out on staff paper, then draw a 2nd above and below the Cs.

- Improvise a piece using these Cs and the keys around them.

and crossing the right hand over and back as you play the other Cs. How would you notate this?

Play B-C-D-C in the middle C area. Use fingers 2-3-4-3 of the right hand. Now cross the left hand over the right hand and play those keys up an octave. Use fingers 4-3-2-3 in the left hand.

Play D-C-B-C the same way, using the opposite fingers (right hand starts on finger 4, left hand starts on finger 2). Does this remind you of a familiar tune?

> ·············· *GREEN ● LIGHT* ··············
>
> Have some fun doing the crossovers! Choose the notes you want to play, leave one hand in a given spot straight in front of you, and cross the other hand over to the octave above or below, then two octaves above and below. Play this again, keeping the damper pedal down. Experiment playing softly and loudly.

A "C" Piece

M.A. Martin

- Here is my piece using the Cs.

- Look at the notation for crossing over, either left hand over right hand, or right hand over left hand.

EIGHTH NOTES

Expand your rhythmic knowledge by dividing the basic beat

The basic beat is the quarter note. Two eighth notes fill the same time as one quarter note. You can feel this division by clapping "Jingle Bells."

You can count out loud by saying, "One-uh, two-uh, three-uh, four-uh," for one full measure of eighth notes in 4/4 time. You can also say, "One-and, two-and." If you are familiar with,

"ti-ti-tah," you can count the quarter notes as "tah" and the eighth notes as "ti-ti, ti-ti."

Nursery rhymes are a great source of metered rhythms. If you say the words to "Hot Cross Buns," you can then count them as:

Hot cross buns, hot cross buns,

Seeing the Rhythm

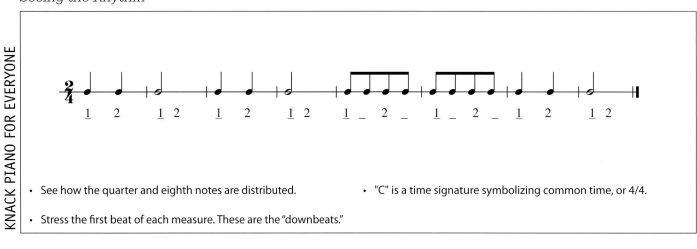

- See how the quarter and eighth notes are distributed.

- Stress the first beat of each measure. These are the "downbeats."

- "C" is a time signature symbolizing common time, or 4/4.

Track 19

Eighth Notes as Singles and Groups

- The single eighth note has a flag to differentiate it from a quarter note.

- Groups of eighth notes can be beamed together. How many you beam will help the performer read the rhythm.

Tah tah tah-ah, tah tah tah-ah
1   2   3-4 1   2   3-4
One a pen-ny, two a pen-ny,
Ti ti ti-ti ti ti ti ti
1 uh 2-uh 3 uh 4- uh
Hot cross buns.
Tah tah tah-ah
1   2   3-4

MAKE IT EASY

Some music instruction has linked the quarter notes with "walking," and the eighth notes with "running." Whatever helps you to understand and to reproduce the rhythms is a good thing. Feel the beat, feel the rhythm.

"Oh! Susanna" with Eighth Notes

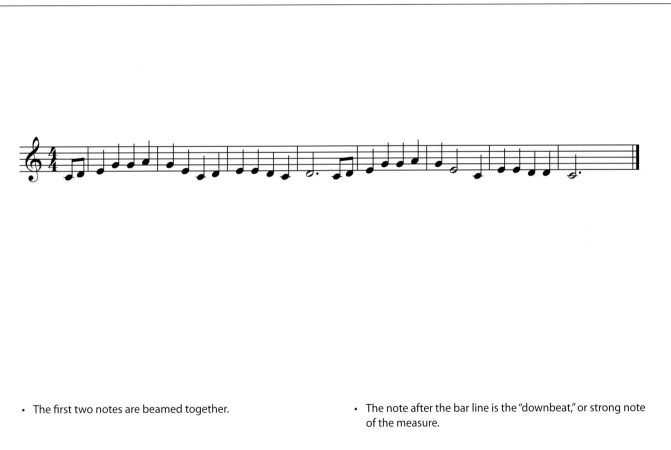

- The first two notes are beamed together.

- The note after the bar line is the "downbeat," or strong note of the measure.

MAJOR FIVE-FINGER PATTERNS
Get accustomed to more detailed topography

The words "major" and "minor" are very familiar when you think of music. They also pertain to a particular feel on the keyboard. Hearing the sound and feeling the pattern on the piano will reinforce your knowledge of major and minor music.

You'll hear major sounds in the song "Doe, a Deer"; in (perhaps) the vocal exercise your chorus sings; and in "Ode to Joy," "Old Macdonald," and "Camptown Races."

Being able to play a major five-finger pattern starting on any key, black or white, with each hand, then with hands together, will increase your knowledge, your ear, and your technique.

The sound of major relates to the pattern—from a given note play up a whole step, up another whole step, then play

C Major Five-finger Pattern

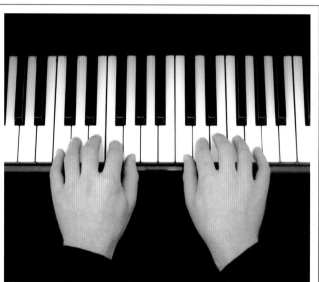

- All the keys are white.

- The thumb is close to the outer edge of the white key, touching the key with only the side of the tip.

- The thumb is slanted slightly toward the wrist. When the thumb is pre-

pared, the other fingers must curve.

- To be comfortable and keep the wrists straight, sit back on the bench so your arms are not crowded, or play right hand up an octave, left hand down an octave.

- The half step is marked with a slur.

- These five notes are the first five notes of the C major scale.

up a half step, then a whole step. It can be illustrated like this:

1 2 3 4 5.

On the keyboard this pattern makes the topography different when beginning on various keys. There are "twins," however! C major and G major five-finger patterns use all white keys. D major and A major five-finger patterns use white keys except for the 3rd fingers, which are on black keys F♯ and C♯ respectively.

··········· **GREEN ● LIGHT** ···········

Find and play all the five-finger patterns, starting on each white key. Use one finger until you have the topographical pattern figured out. Then try playing it with the right hand, 1-2-3-4-5, then the left hand, 5-4-3-2-1. Think about the arrangement of black and white keys, and about which patterns are more difficult to play and why they are more difficult.

D Major Five-finger Pattern

- Prepare 3rd fingers on F♯, wrists slightly elevated.

- Lower the wrists a bit as you place the other fingers on their keys.

- Make sure the thumb plays only on the side of the tip, and slants toward the wrist.

- The half step is marked with a slur.

- The five notes are five consecutive letters.

- The black key must be called F-sharp (and not G-flat) because it is in the place of F natural.

PLAYING FIVE-FINGER PATTERNS

Strengthen each finger and the palm of the hand to build a strong unit for playing

Learning and remembering the pattern of half and whole steps makes it possible to play a major five-finger pattern starting on any key. The relevant point is the location of the half step. It is between the 3rd and 4th degrees (steps) as you start UP the pattern. Another way to think of it, which helps no matter which direction you play, is to locate the half step

above the 3rd finger. To help you play the pattern, relax your hand above the keys and prepare the black keys (if there are black keys) first.

Once you know the keys in a pattern, play each finger gently and hold for three counts. You can do this for one hand at a time, then hands together using the same finger

D Major Five-finger Pattern

- The 3rd finger prepares its black key, F♯, first.

- The hand is slightly elevated, then the other fingers go on the white keys comfortably. The wrist lowers slightly.

- Notice that all the fingers are touching their keys. Press each key from this position; don't lift the finger in order to play.

- Play each key gently so that the other fingers don't have to "help."

D Major, Thumb Side of Hand

- Thumb plays on the side of the tip, and slants slightly toward the wrist.

- The thumb and 2nd finger form a relaxed "C" shape.

- Because there is a black key in the pattern, it is prepared first so that the other fingers can be arranged comfortably on the white keys.

numbers—i.e. both pinkies or fifth fingers. This is called contrary motion.

Next, play the pattern hands together starting with the lowest key. The only fingers with the same numbers that play together are the third fingers. This is called parallel motion.

Remember to prepare any black keys first; then the other fingers place themselves comfortably on the white keys. "Comfortable" is the important word. The wrist and thumb should be relaxed.

Sometimes, the fourth finger will be on a black key. It's even more important to prepare it first; then the pinky finger can be aligned close to it.

When you have finished with the patterns beginning on white keys, find the patterns that begin on a black key! The fingering will be the same; it will feel differently because you probably are not used to fingers 5 and 1 being on black keys. Go slowly, play the pattern with one finger (finger 2 is best), and when you have it figured out, play it with 1-2-3-4-5, or 5-4-3-2-1.

A Five Finger Exercise in C and D

M.A. Martin

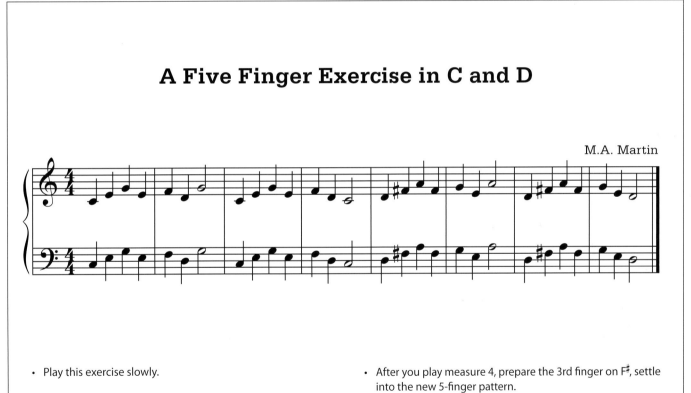

- Play this exercise slowly.

- The hand and wrist should feel relaxed after playing each key.

- After you play measure 4, prepare the 3rd finger on F♯, settle into the new 5-finger pattern.

MINOR FIVE-FINGER PATTERNS
Time to create interest in your journey; bring on the trolls

The sound of minor is quite dramatic. "In the Hall of the Mountain King" by Grieg, Beethoven's Fifth Symphony, the verse of "We Three Kings," Mozart's 40th Symphony, the theme from "Inspector Gadget," Tchaikovsky's "Sugar Plum Fairy," "Stairway to Heaven"; these are all melodies that you can connect with the minor sound.

The arrangement of whole and half steps is only a little different from the major pattern, but oh, what a difference in the sound! The half step in a minor five-finger pattern lies between degrees two and three. It can be illustrated like this:

1 23 4 5.

Another way, no matter what direction you go, is to locate the half step below the 3rd finger.

C Minor Five-finger Pattern

- 3rd fingers are on black keys, E-flat.

- In the left hand, the half step is felt between fingers 4 and 3. In the right hand, the half step is felt between fingers 2 and 3.

- Play up and down the pattern with one finger, then

with fingers 1-2-3-4-5, or 5-4-3-2-1.

- Now move the 3rd finger UP a half step and play the C major pattern.

- Play one after another several times, especially if at first you cannot tell the difference.

- You need a flat sign in front of the E to make this pattern minor. Now the 3rd finger is on a black key.

- Find three places on each staff where half steps occur

naturally (no sharps or flats involved).

- Play them and remember the key names.

To change a major five-finger pattern to a minor one, move the 3rd finger, both hands, down a half step. Now you see the half step below the 3rd finger. In major, the half step is above the 3rd finger.

ZOOM

The other term for "five-finger pattern" is "penta-scale," meaning five steps, or five notes. This should be differentiated from the "pentatonic scale," which means the division of an octave into five degrees or steps. The sound of the pentatonic scale is heard by playing the five black keys on the piano.

D Minor Five-finger Pattern

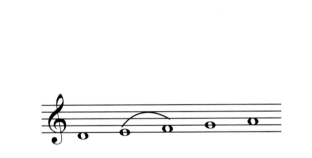

- All fingers are on white keys.

- If it doesn't feel comfortable to play this, sit farther back on your bench, or play right hand up an octave, or left hand down an octave.

- Your fingers are slightly away from the black keys;

you have to be conscious of an elevated palm (it's like a dome), and a slanted thumb.

- Play up and down the pattern; then move the 3rd finger up a half step to F♯. All the fingers move slightly forward to accommodate this.

- A flat or a natural sign is not needed for this minor pattern.

- Five different, consecutive letter names are necessary for a five-finger pattern.

- After playing and listening to the pattern, move the 3rd fingers to F♯. Play up and down the pattern and listen to the different sound.

65

TOPOGRAPHY OF PATTERNS
They don't all look alike or feel alike, but they sound alike

Getting to know the arrangement of black and white keys for the major and minor five-finger patterns is a good aid to finding your way around the keyboard.

It's easy to remember the C and G major patterns. They feel exactly the same; the half step comes between two white keys. Keep your fingers away from the black keys when you play these.

To change C and G patterns to minor, move the 3rd fingers down a half step. Now both 3rd fingers are on black keys (E♭ or B♭, respectively), and the other fingers move slightly forward to accommodate this.

Two other patterns that begin on white keys are twins—D major and A major. In this pattern 3rd fingers are on black keys (F♯ and C♯). To change the D and A major patterns to

C and G Major "Twin" Patterns

- The thumb is slanted, and the fingers are away from the black keys; the 2nd finger needs to curve a little more to play equally with the thumb.

- These patterns use all white keys because of the place-ment of the "gaps," where there are no black keys.

- If you play these patterns at the same time, you will hear an interesting sound!

D and A Major "Twin" Patterns

- 3rd fingers are on the front edges of the black keys F♯ and C♯.

- Fingers 1, 2, 4, and 5 are comfortably placed on white keys.

- Play the right hand up and down its pattern; play slowly and gently. Feel the depth of the "keybed."

minor, move the 3rd fingers down a half step. Now all the fingers are on white keys!

Now for the *really* different patterns. E major goes up from E to F♯, G♯, A, and B. Be sure to prepare the black keys first, especially in the left hand. Notice when the LH goes from E to F♯, the 4th and 3rd fingers are on black keys.

The same situation occurs in the right hand in the F major five-finger pattern. The only black key in this pattern is B-flat, and the 4th finger plays it. Prepare finger 4 first, then let the other fingers fall comfortably on C (pinky), A (3rd finger, which

will probably be between the black keys), G (2nd finger very near the black keys) and F (thumb, playing on the side of the tip, and slanting toward the wrist). In the left hand, finger 2 feels the B♭ first; then the other fingers relax on their keys.

E Major and F Major Five-finger Patterns

- Notice the placement of the left hand finger 5, and right hand finger 5—a little closer to the black keys to accommodate finger 4 (LH) on F♯ and finger 4 (RH) on B♭.

- All other fingers are arranged comfortably on their keys.

- These are not meant to be played simultaneously. You may, but be ready for a very dissonant (discordant) sound.

B Major Five-finger Pattern

- This pattern feels the most uncomfortable at first!

- The left hand thumb and the right hand pinky are prepared first, on the front edges of the black keys; then LH 3 and 4, RH 3 and 2.

- The other fingers fit comfortably (or as comfort-ably as can be!) on their white keys by moving the hands forward toward the fallboard.

- Keep arms and wrist straight; don't twist arms to the left or the right. Go forward in order to fit comfortably.

THE MAJOR/MINOR PATTERNS
Five-finger patterns help you learn the keyboard and strengthen fingers/hands

You can practice the five-finger patterns several ways. First, practice the C or D major/minor patterns. I like to do this exercise hands together. Play the same finger numbers in each hand three times, holding the last repetition gently. Set a strong rhythmic pulse. Say, "one-two-ho-old," for each

finger. Begin the exercise on a different finger each day, but be sure to play all the fingers. If this first pattern was major, change it to minor by moving the third fingers down a half step. You can do as many as you have time for. Always feel relaxed in the wrist—the firm parts of the hands are the

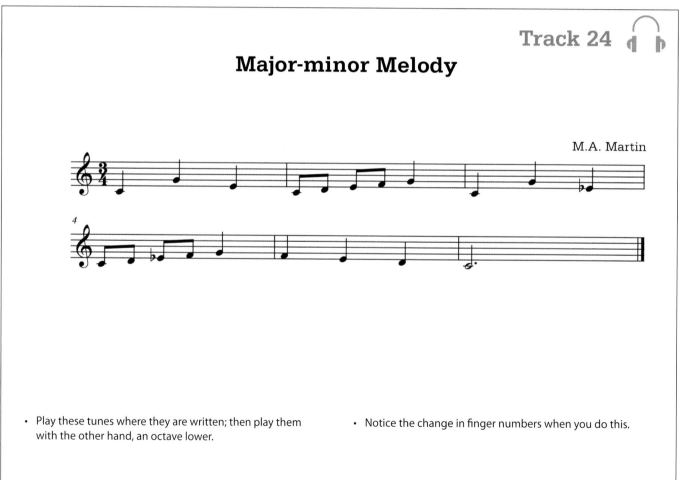

- Play these tunes where they are written; then play them with the other hand, an octave lower.
- Notice the change in finger numbers when you do this.

fingertips. Check the thumbs to be sure they are slightly slanted from the side of the tips up to the wrists (which are parallel to the floor).

When you have done C and G, D and A patterns, change to a hands-separately routine. The E, F, and B patterns are very different in each hand and you will need to concentrate on one hand at a time. Vary your playing by starting at the top of the pattern and playing down and up.

When playing feels very easy, play the patterns hands together in parallel motion. This means you are playing both hands in the same direction; different fingers will play together, except for the 3rd finger. Again, play slowly and feel the depth you need to play each key to reach the "keybed."

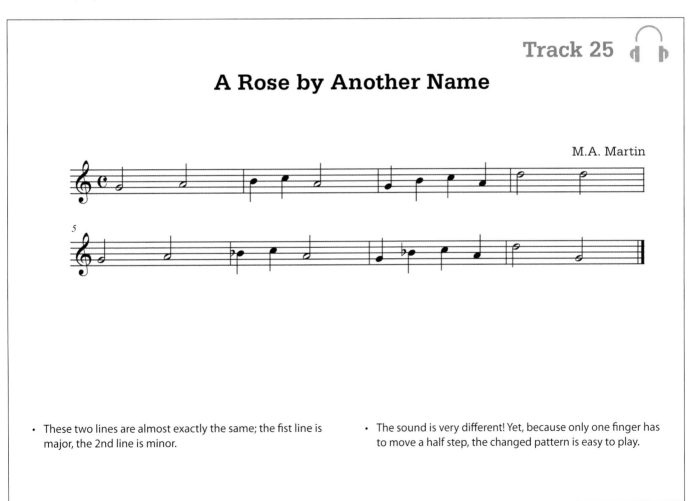

Track 25

A Rose by Another Name

M.A. Martin

- These two lines are almost exactly the same; the fist line is major, the 2nd line is minor.

- The sound is very different! Yet, because only one finger has to move a half step, the changed pattern is easy to play.

FROM PATTERNS TO CHORDS!
The major and minor five-finger patterns are useful for finding chords

What is a chord? It is simply three or more notes played at once. To our Western ears, chords built with intervals of 3rds sound great. The basics of chord building start with forming triads, or three-note/key chords. The chords for the patterns are played with every other key/note/finger (5-3-1 or 1-3-5). Visually on the keyboard this is pretty easy; visually on the

staff, chords are easy to write and to see (line-note, line-note, line-note, or space-note, space-note, space-note); but technically, these chords are not easy to play. Be sure to work with one hand at a time.

Chords are built up from a lower note, which is called the "root." Choose a key, G for instance, and go up a 3rd to B, then

G Major Blocked Chord

- The hand is over a G major five-finger pattern.

- Fingers 5-3-1 play the G major triad. Say the names of the keys in this triad, up and down: G-B-D-B-G.

- Since there are no black keys to play, keep the fingers slightly away from the black keys.

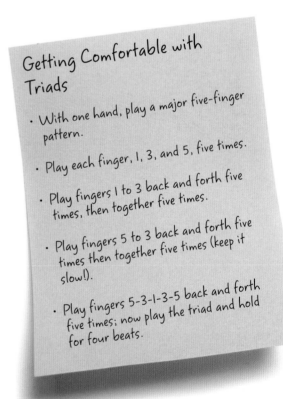

Getting Comfortable with Triads

- With one hand, play a major five-finger pattern.

- Play each finger, 1, 3, and 5, five times.

- Play fingers 1 to 3 back and forth five times, then together five times.

- Play fingers 5 to 3 back and forth five times then together five times (keep it slow!).

- Play fingers 5-3-1-3-5 back and forth five times; now play the triad and hold for four beats.

up another 3rd to D. This last note is a 5th above the root. Go up another 3rd to F. This is a 7th above the root. A chord which has four different notes, a 3rd apart, is called a seventh chord.

You are not expected to play a seventh chord with one hand! If you want to hear the sound (and it's a nice one), play two notes in each hand. Investigate the different sounds you can make with these seventh chords by playing on every key for one octave.

ZOOM

Chord patterns can be blocked (played simultaneously), or broken (played one note at a time). Listen to our National Anthem, which begins with a broken-chord passage. When a broken chord is extended to include the next chord up an octave (G-B-D, up to G-B-D), it is called an "arpeggio." Try playing this chord hand over hand.

CHORDS

G Minor Blocked Chord

- The hand is over a G minor five-finger pattern.

- Fingers 1-3-5 play the G minor triad. Say the names of the keys in the chord, up and down: G-B♭-D-B♭-G.

- Since there is a black key, prepare the 3rd finger over the black key, then place

the other fingers comfortably around it.

- Practice the chord as suggested—each finger alone, then two fingers in combination, then three fingers.

B Major Blocked Chord

- The wrists and arms are straight.

- The black-key-fingers, LH 1 and RH 5, are on the front edge of F♯.

- This is not an easy chord position to play. Experiment with fingers 4-2-1 in the left hand, fingers 1-2-4 in the right hand.

71

BLOCKED & BROKEN TRIADS

These translate to other chording instruments—guitar, accordion, organ, ukulele, mandolin

In a melody, intervals of 2nds refer to scale-like passages. Intervals of 3rds, 4ths, 5ths, and 6ths refer to chord-like passages. Recognizing these chordal passages helps in the reading of music.

In the lower part of the keyboard (or in the upper part if the melody is in the low section), or on stringed instruments like guitar and ukulele, chords add an accompaniment to a melody. The chords can be blocked (or "solid"), or they can be broken (or "arpeggiated").

You can play a G major chord in the left hand to accompany

Track 26

Chords

M.A. Martin

Piano

- Here is a simple tune using blocked and broken chords in both hands.
- Remember to name the first note in each hand; then read by intervals the rest of the way.

the tune, "Are You Sleeping." The melody begins on G, goes up a 2nd, up a 2nd, down a 3rd. Then it repeats the pattern. Practice that portion of the tune, and when it is easy, accompany it with the G major chord; play it on the word, "Are."

Now choose one particular chord, get both hands ready on it, an octave apart, and play it broken from the lowest note to the highest note. End with both hands playing the chord blocked. Try this with all the major chords you can play; then change each chord to minor. On another day, press the damper pedal and play the arpeggio. It makes a full and rich sound!

You can play "Oh, When the Saints" on a major chord position. Let's use C major for our example. The tune begins by playing C up to E, then F to G. The intervals are up a 3rd, up a 2nd, up a 2nd. Repeat this phrase. Play it again a third time, but extend the phrase by playing down the chord to C, back up to E, down a 2nd to D. Can you "pick out" the rest of the tune? You don't have to move out of the five-finger pattern.

Track 27

Oh, When the Saints

Traditional

- I have written out "Oh, When the Saints."

- I put chords in the left hand, in case you want to try it.

- A good workout for the left hand is to play the melody an octave or two lower.

INTERVALS: 6THS
To make a simple accompaniment, play 5ths and 6ths

The easiest accompaniment for a melody (assuming it is a simple, rather short melody) is a blocked 5th. This means that you can play "Are You Sleeping" again, but the left hand plays only the outside keys of the G major chord. It is easier to play, and in some cases sounds better. With this pattern, the tune goes, G-A-B-G, G-A-B-G, B-C-D, B-C-D.

Play the tune on the C major five-finger pattern—it feels the same but sounds either higher or lower. (C-D-E-C, C-D-E-C, E-F-G, E-F-G). The outside 5th in the left hand includes the notes C up to G.

You can make the accompaniment more interesting by moving to the interval of a 6th. This involves moving the thumb up a whole step, or the fingers away from the thumb. Stay in the C major five-finger pattern for the melody; play

Right Hand Plays a 6th

- The only gap is between fingers 1 and 2.

- Play back and forth between the 5th and the 6th by moving only the thumb.

- Play the 5th changing to a 6th at least seven times, by moving fingers away from the thumb.

Left Hand Plays a 6th

- The only gap is between thumb and finger 2.

- Play back and forth between the 5th and the 6th, first by moving the

thumb, then by moving the fingers away from the thumb.

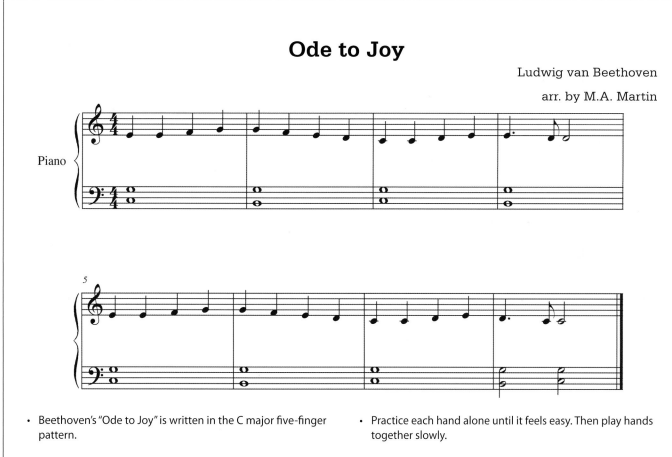

"Ode to Joy" by Beethoven. Start on E in the right hand. The first phrase of the tune consists of 2nds only. Once you have the melody in your fingers, try accompanying with first a blocked 5th, then a 6th. Can you hear where to make the change from 5th to 6th?

Change to the 6th by moving the thumb up; then play the 6th by moving the fingers away from the thumb. The 6th is made of either C up to A, or B up to G.

Which 6th sounds better with your melody?

Accompany each note of the five-finger pattern with either a 5th or a 6th. You need to play ultra slowly so you can manage the left hand accompaniment. When this is manageable, switch hands—five-finger pattern in the left hand, 5ths and 6ths in the right hand.

CHORDS

Ode to Joy

Ludwig van Beethoven

arr. by M.A. Martin

Piano

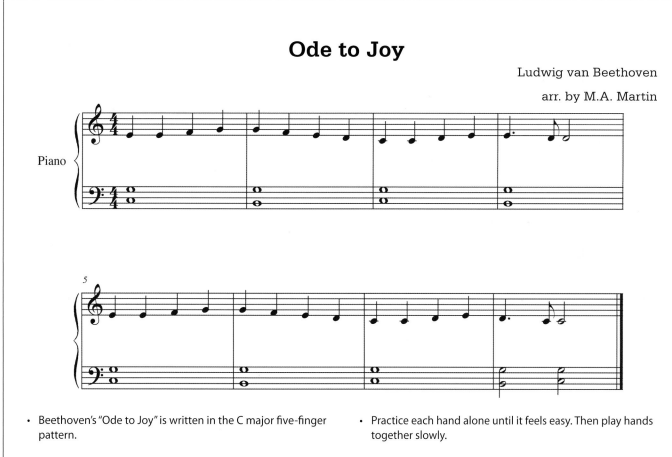

- Beethoven's "Ode to Joy" is written in the C major five-finger pattern.

- The left hand plays 5ths and 6ths as accompaniment.

- Practice each hand alone until it feels easy. Then play hands together slowly.

FIRST INVERSION
It can be easier to play a chord that has been inverted

The triads you have learned so far sound good, but sometimes inverting the chords makes a better sound, and might be easier to play. Learning to play triads in root position (the name of the chord is the lowest note), then playing an inversion, makes you feel at ease at the keyboard. Also, seeing the inversion on the staff in a blocked, then broken form, enables you to see chord patterns in any kind of music.

Since there are three different notes in a triad, there will be three positions of the chord. In the root position, the name of the chord will be the lowest note. The triad stacks up in intervals of 3rds.

Take the lowest note and make it the top note (up an octave from the low position). If your chord is a C major chord, the lowest note will now be E, the middle note G, and the highest

C Major Chord, First Inversion, LH

- The intervals between the keys have changed: the outside keys are a 6th apart; the interval between fingers 1 and 3 is a 4th.

- Play back and forth between the root position chord and the first inversion chord, blocked and broken.

- Sing or say the names of the notes in the chord, up and down.

C Major Chord, First Inversion, RH

- The shape of the chord is the same as in the LH, but the most relaxed fingering is 1-2-5.

- Remember that the gap in the 6th is between fingers 1 and 2. This explains the fingering.

- Play back and forth between the root position chord and the first inversion, blocked and broken chords.

- Sing or say the names of the notes in the chord as you play.

76

note, C. The intervallic structure changed from all 3rds to a 3rd from the bottom key to the middle key, and a 4th from the middle key up to the highest key. The outside interval changed from a 5th to a 6th.

Again, take the lowest note, E, and move it to the top (up an octave). G is now the lowest key, C is in the middle, and E is the top key. The outside interval is a 6th.

You should practice these different positions of a chord, singing or saying the names of the keys as you play them.

Play them in the left hand, then in the right hand.

C Major Chord, 1st Inversion

- I have written the first inversion of the C major chord, first in a broken form, then a blocked form.

- Practice this inversion as you did the root position chord, both hands, an octave apart. Play left hand from bottom to top, right hand the same; then play them blocked.

SECOND INVERSION
With this inversion, play all the bugle tunes you know

In this inversion, the intervals shift once again. The outside keys still form a 6th, but the 4th and the 3rd have switched places. The fingering in the left hand is now 5-2-1; in the right hand it is 1-3-5.

If you can hum, whistle, or simply hear bugle tunes, you should be able to pick out "Reveille," "Taps," or any other bugle tune, when your hand is on the second inversion. You will need the other hand to play a fourth key, which will be up a 3rd, or an octave above the lowest key in the inversion. If you go to baseball games, you can hear the organist play up the 2nd inversion, with that added octave at the top: G-C-E-G-E-G.

Using the 2nd inversion of the chord, you can also play the first phrase of "Eine Kleine Nachtmusik" by Mozart. Begin with

C Major Chord, Second Inversion, LH

- The bottom G and the top E form a 6th.

- With the gap between fingers 1 and 2, the middle note, C is played with finger 2.

- Practice moving from root position to first inversion to second inversion, always slowly, always going up, then down.

- After you have played the inversions blocked, play them broken, slowly, but with a steady beat.

- Play chord inversions down, from the top note. Naming the notes as you play helps.

C Major Chord, Second Inversion, RH

- With fingers 1 and 5 on the 6th, finger 3 naturally plays the middle key, C.

- Practice this inversion in conjunction with the first inversion and the root position. Go up the keyboard, naming the notes of the chord from the lowest to the highest.

- Now play the chords arpeggiated from lowest to highest. Play slowly and keep a steady beat. Name the notes as you play them.

- When you play down the chords, start with the top note. Keep naming notes as you play.

78

the middle note, C, and play down to G, back up to C, repeat three times and extend the phrase by playing up to E and the next G.

Once your mind and ear start working, you might hear lots of other tune fragments.

CHORDS

• The 2nd inversion chord is written in the treble clef.

• "Taps" is written out for you to experiment with.

TRIADS WITH BLACK KEYS

Having black keys in a chord makes it easy to find and feel the chord

Black keys once again help with finding your place on the keyboard! When you play the D major triad in root position, then invert the chord, you are able to feel the place. Experiment with fingering: When you play the first inversion of the D major triad in the left hand, finger 5 doesn't always feel comfortable on F♯. Try playing the F♯ with finger 4, A with finger 2, and D with finger 1.

In the right hand, if the 5th finger is on a black key (F♯ in the D major chord), you can try the same fingering; i.e. finger 4 on F♯, finger 2 on D, finger 1 on A.

Personally, I like to use the thumb on all the chords, whether it plays a white key or a black key. You can try other fingerings,

C Minor Chord, First Inversion, Both Hands

- The fingers used here are the same as an all-white-key chord, LH 5-3-1, RH 1-2-5.

- Experiment with fingers 1-2-4 when the fifth fingers are on black keys.

- Don't twist the wrist in order to get the thumb on the black key.

- Listen for an even sound. The hand will feel well balanced when the fingers are evenly strong.

C Minor Chord, Second Inversion, Both Hands

- Again, fingers 5-3-1 LH and 1-2-5 RH are used.

- Experiment with other fingerings, but keep using the thumb. It helps keep your hand relaxed.

- Continue to practice one finger at a time; when playing the chord, name each note of the chord.

but don't twist the hand or wrist to get the fingers in place. Move forward toward the fallboard. The goal is comfort and ease of movement.

As with other chord practice, name the notes of the chord as you play them. Saying them aloud helps you to remember them. If you are having trouble playing the chords evenly (all three notes sounding at the same time), go back to the way you worked on each finger, then two-finger combinations.

As the fingers gain strength you will be able to hear a difference in the evenness of the chords.

A Tune of Chord Notes

M.A. Martin

- Analyze this piece for its interval structure. Do you see chords outlined?

- Practice the RH chords blocked, so you can move easily from measure to measure.

- Look for broken chords in LH measure 4. Practice the spot until it feels comfortable.

- Play hands together slowly, blocking chords in RH. Then play slowly as written.

PERFECT 5THS ACCOMPANIMENTS

You can make effective accompaniments with intervals of 5ths, and it's easy!

Start with a melody that uses a familiar five-finger pattern. If the right hand plays the melody, the left hand uses the outside 5th of the same five-finger pattern. Make sure you can play the melody easily before adding an accompaniment. You can play the blocked 5th once, or at the beginning of each measure, or anywhere you like.

The English folk song, "Oranges and Lemons," is a good tune to accompany with 5ths. Play the melody in the right hand, on a G major five-finger pattern.

D B D B G A B C A D B G
Oran-ges and lem-ons, say the bells of St. Clem-ens.
5 3 5 3 1 2 3 4 2 5 3 1

Perfect 5th, White Key to White Key

- Good hand position, slanted thumb, tall pinky.

- The other fingers don't try to help by moving upward. They stay quietly on the keys.

- Play all the white-key-to-white-key 5ths. Play them blocked; then make a little exercise by playing 1-5, 5-1, on each key.

Perfect 5th, Black Key to Black Key

- Fingers 5 and 1, 1 and 5, play on the front edge of the black keys.

- Play softly, keep a good hand position, and hold down each perfect 5th for three or four seconds to get optimum results.

- Play all four black-key-to-black-key perfect 5ths: F♯ to C♯, G♯ to D♯, D♭ to A♭, E♭ to B♭.

- Play the 5ths blocked, hands separately; then play the exercise, 1-5, 5-1.

Practice the melody until it feels easy. Then place the left hand on the G major five-finger pattern, but prepare to play only the outside 5th with fingers 5 and 1. When you play the melody again, play the left hand simultaneously with the first note of the right hand. Hold it throughout the phrase. Then play both hands again.

You can practice playing the two hands together like this on any five-finger pattern, major or minor. Help the left hand become more adept by switching the melody to the left hand and the accompanying 5th to the right hand.

Perfect 5th, White Key to Black Key

- The wrists and arms remain straight.

- Move forward on the keys to get the thumb or pinky on its key.

- This position helps you to play the B major five-finger pattern.

Perfect 5th, Black Key to White Key

- The wrists and arms remain straight.

- Move forward on the keys to get the thumb or pinky on its key.

- Now you are ready to play the B♭ major five-finger pattern. Hands separately, play up the pattern.

- Remember, the half step is above the 3rd finger.

PERFECT 5THS, ETC.

CHROMATIC SCALE IN PERFECT 5THS

The chromatic scale consists of every key in the octave, nothing skipped

It's fun to play every key on the keyboard, or every key in an octave. This is called a chromatic scale. An easy fingering for this scale is to play only finger 3 on the black keys, finger 1 on the white keys, except in the gaps where there is no black key. In the gaps play fingers 1-2 (right hand going up, left hand going down), or in the opposite direction, fingers

2-1. You can keep your three strongest fingers close together as you slowly ascend in the right hand, starting on E: 1-2-3-1-3-1-3-1-2-3-1-3-1. Use the same fingering in the left hand, starting on C, and descending to the next C.

After you have experimented playing the chromatic scale in single notes, try playing it in perfect 5ths. It may feel awkward

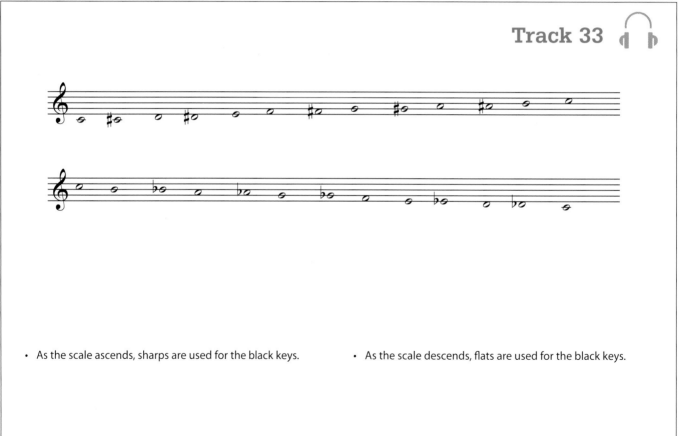

Track 33

- As the scale ascends, sharps are used for the black keys.

- As the scale descends, flats are used for the black keys.

at first because fingers one and five play these 5ths, whether they are on black keys or white keys.

As you try out this chromatic scale in 5ths, you'll find that most of the blocked 5ths are black to black keys or white to white keys. When B or B♭ is the lower key, and F♯ or F is the higher key, it is a combination interval—a combination of black key and white key. It is a little trickier to play, but just remember to keep your wrist and arm straight.

Play the chromatic scale in perfect 5ths with the left hand, then the right hand. When you feel at ease with this, try

playing both hands simultaneously, one octave apart.

Play only the 5ths up and down chromatically, holding each one for two beats. This sounds vaguely like the classic James Bond theme. I wonder if you can alter some notes and make it sound more like the theme?

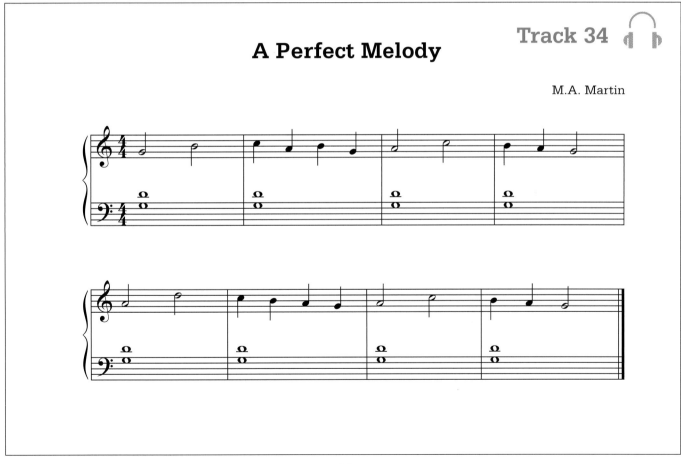

A Perfect Melody

M.A. Martin

PERFECT 5THS, ETC.

DOTTED QUARTER & EIGHTH NOTES

We will add some refinement to our melody, and to the National Anthem

We have seen that a dot beside the half note gives it an extra beat. The purpose of the dot beside the note is to add length to that note by half the value of the note. By that definition, a dotted quarter note will get a beat and a half. The second half of the dot is usually followed by an eighth note.

The easiest tune with which to illustrate this is "London Bridge." Clap the rhythm, holding the syllable, "Lon-" a little longer, then saying the syllable, "don" rather quickly:

Lo-on-don Bridge is fal-ling down . . .
1-2 uh   3   4 1 2 3-4

The "tie" is another way to write this rhythm. A tie joins two notes of the same pitch; they form a single sound that lasts as

Familiar Examples of ♩. ♪ (or Dotted Quarter and 8th Notes)

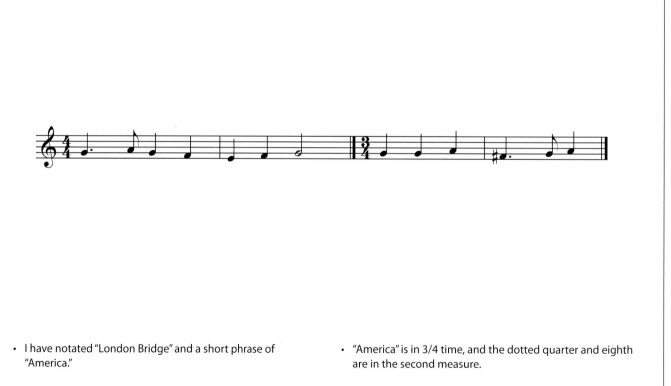

- I have notated "London Bridge" and a short phrase of "America."

- The dotted quarter and eighth notes take up two beats in the first measure of the 4/4 tune.

- "America" is in 3/4 time, and the dotted quarter and eighth are in the second measure.

long as the two notes together. "London Bridge" begins with a quarter note tied to an eighth note, followed by a single eighth note. The feel is the same, but the dot takes less ink—an important consideration 300 years ago!

"America" is another song that uses a dotted quarter and eighth note. It is in 3/4 time, and the dotted note comes on the words, "'tis" and "liberty."

My coun-try, 'tis of thee, sweet land of li-ber-ty, etc.

Sing this song and feel the longer notes on "'tis" and the first syllable of "liberty," followed by the quick notes on "of" and the second syllable of "liberty." Our National Anthem starts with a dotted eighth note followed by a sixteenth note. Those two notes fill the time of one quarter-note beat. Try singing or saying the words in rhythm, in order to feel the rhythmic pattern. The song is in three-quarter time.

Dotted Quarter and 8th Notes, Dotted 8th and 16th Notes or ♩. ♪ and ♫

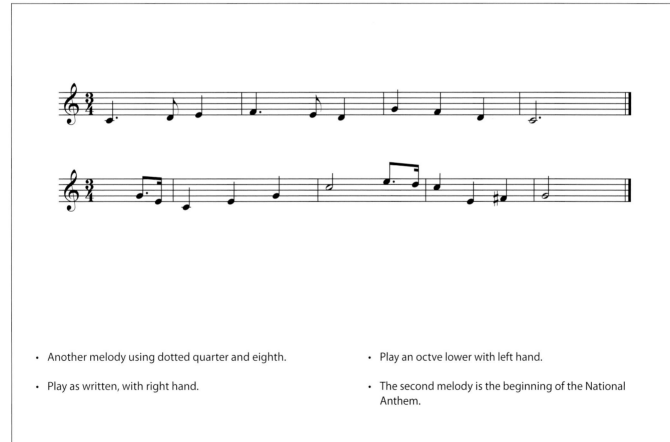

- Another melody using dotted quarter and eighth.

- Play as written, with right hand.

- Play an octve lower with left hand.

- The second melody is the beginning of the National Anthem.

"OH! SUSANNA" AGAIN...

Using the dotted quarter and eighth notes to make the tune more authentic

We have reached the final stage of "Oh! Susanna" and it is almost like the original. The tune is written here in 4/4 time and begins with a dotted quarter note followed by an eighth note.

The two notes over the word, "I," constitute two full beats. In other words, the song begins on beat three. In the first full

measure, the last two notes form the dotted quarter/eighth pattern.

After you have practiced this melody slowly, try the accompanied version—melody in the right hand, perfect 5ths in the left hand.

Stephen Foster was born in 1826 near Pittsburgh, Penn-

- The melody of "Oh! Susanna" written out using dotted quarter and eighth notes.

sylvania. "Oh! Susanna" was his first hit song; it was made popular by the minstrel shows of that era.

PERFECT 5THS, ETC.

Oh! Susanna

S. Foster

- After you have practiced the melody and it is easy to play, play this version, with an accompaniment in the left hand.

TRIPLETS IN MUSIC
From an Irish jig to Humpty Dumpty

Sometimes the basic beat is divided into three eighth notes instead of two—this is called a triplet. A perfect example is the famous "March" from Tchaikovsky's Nutcracker. The second beat of the first measure is a triplet. Counting out loud, you can say, "One, two-ah-la, three, four," or "Tah, tri-ple-tee, tah, tah," or "Tah, tak-a-tee, tah, tah."

Some music divides every beat into triplets; this is called compound meter. When the time signature has eight as the bottom number, it is compound meter. It is called compound because you feel the beat two ways: 6/8 has six eighth notes in a measure, and it can be counted that way. But it usually implies a faster beat; i.e. two long beats divided into triplets. In dance music these are called "jigs." "The Irish Washerwoman" is a good example. The nursery rhymes "Humpty,

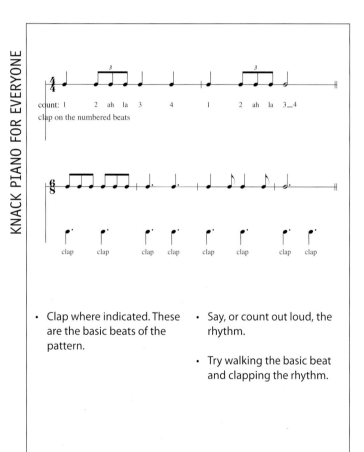

count: 1   2 ah la   3   4   1   2 ah la 3_4
clap on the numbered beats

clap   clap   clap clap   clap   clap   clap   clap

- Clap where indicated. These are the basic beats of the pattern.
- Say, or count out loud, the rhythm.
- Try walking the basic beat and clapping the rhythm.

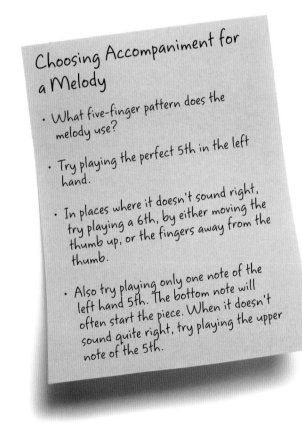

Choosing Accompaniment for a Melody

- What five-finger pattern does the melody use?
- Try playing the perfect 5th in the left hand.
- In places where it doesn't sound right, try playing a 6th, by either moving the thumb up, or the fingers away from the thumb.
- Also try playing only one note of the left hand 5th. The bottom note will often start the piece. When it doesn't sound quite right, try playing the upper note of the 5th.

KNACK PIANO FOR EVERYONE

Dumpty," "Ride a Cock Horse to Banbury Cross," "Jack and Jill," and "Hickory, Dickory, Dock" make use of triplet rhythm.

The most common compound meters are 6/8, 9/8, and 12/8. In addition to the number of beats indicated by the top number, there are the longer beats (illustrated by the dotted quarter note) of 2, 3, and 4.

Many marches are felt in the triplet rhythm. Even if they have 4/4 as the time signature, they will have triplet figures throughout, such as Tchaikovsky's "March" from the Nutcracker.

There are compound meters with 16 as the bottom note. The sixteenth notes are grouped into triplets, the long beats are dotted eighth notes, and the appropriate time signatures are 3/16, 6/16, 9/16, and 12/16. It is rare, but it is possible also to have 32 as the bottom number.

Triplet-figure Accompaniment

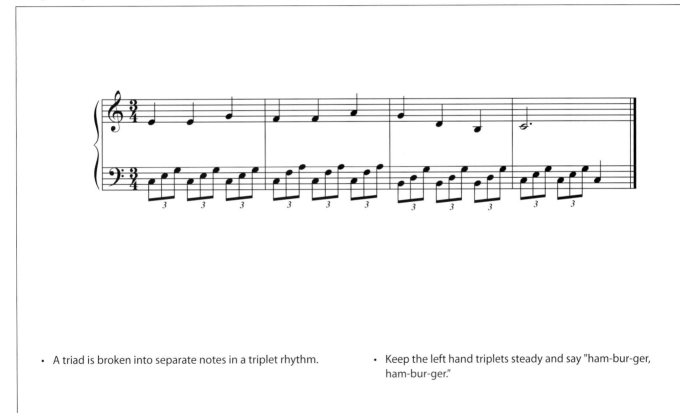

- A triad is broken into separate notes in a triplet rhythm.

- Keep the left hand triplets steady and say "ham-bur-ger, ham-bur-ger."

MORE MUSIC

You are putting it all together, but keep the practice components separate

Here is a good place to stop and take stock of all you have learned. Make a list of the details of music you do not understand. If you cannot find the answers you want in this book, in another book, or from another person, try the Internet.

If you type in "Music Theory" you will get dozens of Web sites. Many of them have quizzes, patterns to clap (with feedback), and chords to fill in. When you type in "Music Notation," you will find interesting discussions on the history of notation, the evolution of the clef signs, and much more. There are also several available articles on the development of the keyboard.

Aside from this, I think feedback is an important element

A "Remember to" List
- Practice the rhythm by clapping or tapping and counting out loud.
- Look through the whole piece and plan the fingering.
- Play slowly, count out loud.
- Play slowly, listening; then play six more times.

- Make sure you are sitting in a good playing position.

- Check your distance from the keyboard, and the height of your bench.

- Your wrists should be floating as if held up by helium baloons.

- You should sit tall, and sit on the front half of the bench or chair.

in your musical training. Find a teacher, or friend who is a music teacher, and let them hear you play, or clap rhythms, or whatever you would like to have reinforced. Record your own playing so you can hear it. You need to be reassured that what you are doing is correct, and that you are relaxed when you play.

Keep attending to your practice schedule. Make sure you are continuing to practice the five-finger patterns and the chords every day—or at least every chance you get. It is the regularity of practicing that gets the job done. I'm convinced once a week doesn't do it—though I guess it's better than nothing!

I hope you have a book of songs or pieces that you can practice, in addition to this one. It is good to have something new to work on every week. It keeps you interested, it helps your practice capabilities, and it can keep you absorbed in this process.

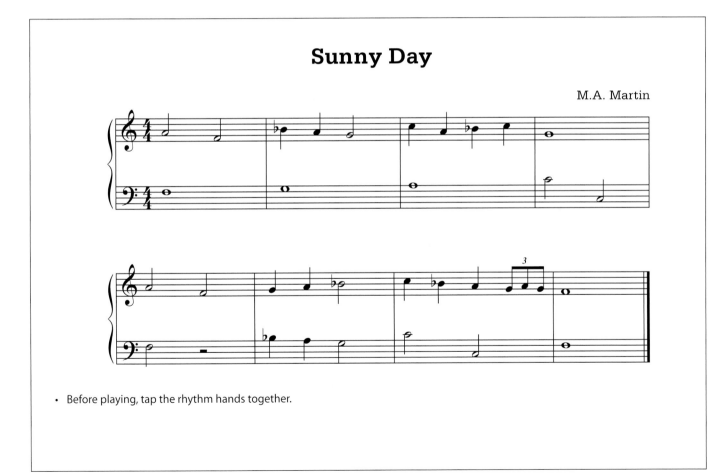

Sunny Day

M.A. Martin

- Before playing, tap the rhythm hands together.

PLAYING A SCALE
The keyboard was made for your hands

What is a scale? It is simply "steps." The octave is divided into twelve different half steps in our European-based music. In other countries the scale is divided into more steps.

Our "Western" music is based on the major-minor system, and each piece of music uses the notes of a particular seven-note scale as a basis. This is the reason why we learn scales and practice scales and chords. Once we learn the patterns in each key,

music reading and playing become so much easier!

Frederic Chopin was not only a famous composer; he was an admired piano teacher. The first scale he taught was the B major scale, and you can see why when you play it. The hand fits naturally over the keys—thumb on the white keys, B and E; fingers 2-3 on the two black keys; fingers 2-3-4 on the three black keys. It is even rather easy to play hands together.

B Major Scale

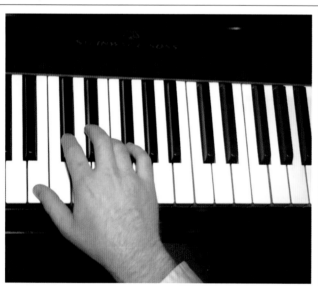

- Fingers 2 and 3 play on the front edge of the two black keys.

- The hand is soft and relaxed.

- The hand and wrist rise and go forward a bit.

- Play back and forth on these two black keys with fingers 2 and 3, rather like you did in the beginning of your music lessons.

Playing the B Major Scale

- The hand turns a little inward to allow the thumb to cross under fingers 2 and 3 and play E.

- The wrist is straight, but relaxed, and the thumb stays slanted toward the wrist.

- Fingers 2 and 3 are quiet on their keys; they are no mov-

ing up to help the thumb.

- Go back and forth between fingers 2 and 3 and thumb crossing under—2-3-1-3-2-3-1-3-2.

- The forearm and elbow move slightly to stay in line with the finger that is playing.

Practice playing the B major scale slowly, starting with one octave up and down. Count two pulses to each note; use the metronome set at 80 to tick the two beats when the scale is comfortable to play. Start the scale practice with one hand at a time; as it becomes easier, play the two hands together.

When you are at ease with the above, play the scale for two octaves up and down, one beat per note (metronome still on 80).

GREEN ● LIGHT

There are two good examples of the major scale descending: The first phrase of the Christmas carol, "Joy to the World," and the first phrase from the Intrada of the "Pas de deux" in The Nutcracker by Tchaikovsky.

- As soon as the thumb plays E, fingers 2-3-4 prepare the three black keys.

- Play E with the thumb, and the three black keys with fingers 2-3-4. Then play back to B: 1-2-3-4-3-2-1-3-2-1.

- Drill this much of the scale five times, until it feels secure.

- The thumb has to cross under finger 4; as the hand turns slightly inward, the elbow moves outward slightly to keep the wrist straight.

- The thumb needs to practice playing this higher B to prepare you for a longer scale passage; otherwise,

finger 5 can end the scale on B.

- Drill the move in which the thumb crosses under finger 4 on A♯: F♯, G♯, A♯, B, A♯, G♯, F♯; or fingers 2-3-4-1-4-3-2.

THE MAJOR SCALE

95

HALF & WHOLE STEPS
The sound came first; the theorists wrote it down later

Why do we like the sound of the major scale so much? Perhaps it has to do with the physics of sound, the overtone series, the regular vibrations our bodies respond to. Whatever the reason, the major scale has come down to us in this form: an octave divided into seven different keys/notes, most of them a whole step apart except between degrees 3 and 4, 7 and 1, which are half steps.

The major sound is associated with *The Sound of Music*, "Edelweiss," the *Star Wars* theme, "Over the Rainbow," "Hey, Mr. Tambourine Man," "Piano Man," Beethoven's "Eroica" Symphony, Mozart's "Eine Kleine Nachtmusik," "Yellow Submarine," and thousands more tunes.

It is time to play the B major scale with both hands simultaneously. Begin with both thumbs on B, an octave apart.

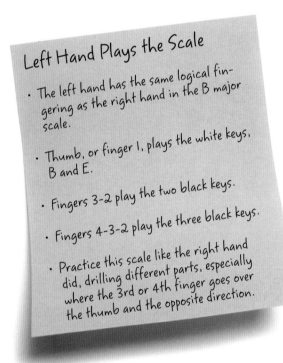

- The names of the keys are written over the dots. Notice the black keys are all sharps.

- The half steps are indicated. All other steps are whole.

- You can play this scale in clusters: thumb plays B; fingers 2-3 play together; then thumb plays E; then fingers 2-3-4 play together; then thumb plays B. This is a good drill to help you feel relaxed as you play the scale.

Left Hand Plays the Scale

- The left hand has the same logical fingering as the right hand in the B major scale.

- Thumb, or finger 1, plays the white keys, B and E.

- Fingers 3-2 play the two black keys.

- Fingers 4-3-2 play the three black keys.

- Practice this scale like the right hand did, drilling different parts, especially where the 3rd or 4th finger goes over the thumb and the opposite direction.

Then play up to the two black keys in a cluster, or together, with fingers 2-3, or 3-2. Both thumbs are ready to play E, then fingers 2-3-4 and 4-3-2 play the three black keys in a cluster. Thumbs end on B. Now proceed down the scale.

All the movements used to play the scale need to be smooth and relaxed, so playing these black key clusters separated by the thumb notes, going up and down, is a beneficial way to practice. As you get more familiar with the scale, notice that the movements are very slight; the upper body keeps in line with the hands and arms so that there is always weight into each key.

In a scale, there must be seven different notes or letter names. When a note is a sharp or flat, that note is a substitute for the natural note/key that is skipped.

B Major Scale on the Staff

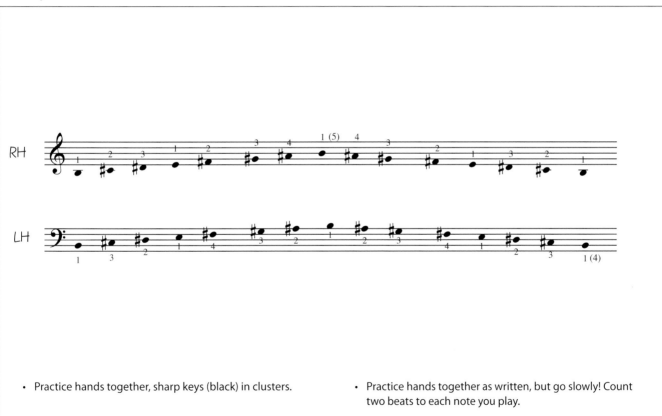

- Practice hands together, sharp keys (black) in clusters.

- Practice hands together as written, but go slowly! Count two beats to each note you play.

THE C MAJOR "TEMPLATE"
You don't need any black keys for this scale

Even though the B major scale is the easiest to play, the C major scale is the easiest in which to see the pattern. It lies naturally on the white keys, with the half steps between degrees 3 and 4, 7 and 1. That is why I like to call it the "template" for the major scale.

When the third finger is on a black key, as in the B major scale, the thumb slips under rather easily. That is because the hand is slightly elevated and the fingers curved to allow the thumb to slip under. When you play the all-white-key scale, keep this in mind. The fingers have to curve a little more to keep the "dome" shape of the hand and the wrist needs to be straight in order for the thumb to slip under finger 3 easily. In order for the thumb to slip under finger 4 easily, the forearm and wrist need to stay in line with the thumb; a slight shifting

C Major Scale—the Template

- The half steps that help to give us the sound of the major scale lie naturally in the gaps where there are no black keys.

- Play this scale with one finger, up and down, to hear the sound.

- Now play the scale with the same fingering you used for the right hand in the B major scale.

- The left hand will use the same fingering as the right hand, but in the opposite direction.

Playing the C Major Scale

- Finger 2 can easily play up and down the C major scale.

- Be sure the left hand plays the scale after the right hand.

- Right hand fingering (ascending) for the scale is usually 1-2-3-1-2-3-4-5.

- The thumb has to slip under the third finger.

- Left hand fingering (ascending) is usually 5-4-3-2-1-3-2-1.

98

of the forearm is called for.

To help get your ear involved, sing the notes of the C major scale with do, re, mi, fa, sol, la, ti, do. Now sing the scale down: do, ti, la, sol, fa, mi, re, do. Notice the "ee" sound of the syllables where the half steps are. Sing "Joy to the World," the first phrase only. Now sing it with the syllables, then with numbers: one, seven, six, five, four, three, two, one. One last time, sing down the scale using the names of the keys: C, B, A, G, F, E, D, C.

ZOOM

Singing with syllables, or solfege, was developed by Guido d'Arezzo in the fourteenth century. The syllables came from a chant in which each phrase started on the next higher note of the scale. Originally the first syllable was "ut." Changing that syllable to "do" and adding the seventh note of the scale are the only differences in the solfege we use today.

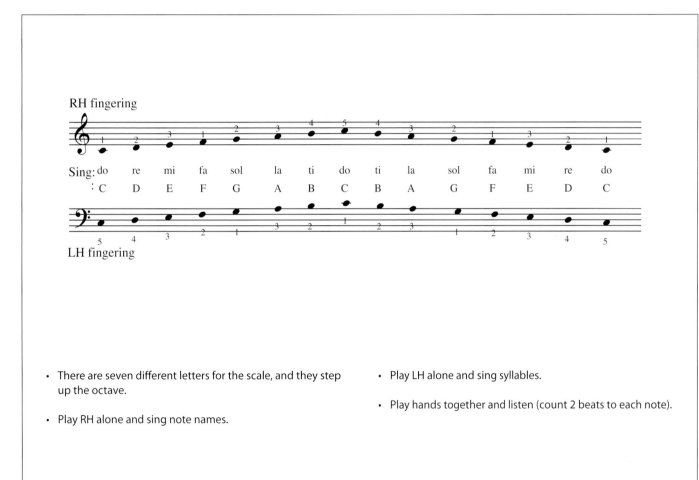

- There are seven different letters for the scale, and they step up the octave.

- Play RH alone and sing note names.

- Play LH alone and sing syllables.

- Play hands together and listen (count 2 beats to each note).

STARTING ON DIFFERENT KEYS
Use the template to play a major scale starting on any key

Begin a scale on D. Keep the C major template in mind: whole steps between all the keys except 3-4, 7-1. Make sure there are seven different consecutive names of keys, D, E, F, G, A, B, C. To keep the template accurate, you must raise F to F♯, and C to C♯. Now it is a major scale!

Most music has home keys—notes that become the center of the music. The home key is stated (in this case, D), the

music wanders around and away from the home key, and the music returns to the home key at the end. This is what we mean when we say that a piece of music is "in the key of D major." Since we almost always sharp the F and the C in music that is in the key of D major, we put those sharps in a key signature at the beginning of each line.

Now you can identify "the key" of a piece if there are no

D Major Scale

- See the two half steps between F♯ and G, C♯ and D.

- Experiment playing only white keys from D to D, then the major scale from D to D. Use one finger only.

- Did you like the sound of the white key scale from D to D? That is called the "Dorian" scale, or mode. It has come down to us, like the major scale, from ancient Greek times, to medieval "church" modes, to modern times.

Playing the D Major Scale

- You can use the same fingering that was suggested for the C major scale; only in this key the fingering is more imperative because of the black keys.

- When the thumb slides under the 3rd finger, the forearm stays in line with the finger that is playing.

- Try playing the Dorian scale with the C major fingering. Remember where the half steps lie (between steps 2 and 3, 6 and 7).

sharps and flats (the key of C major), and if there are two sharps, F# and C# (the key of D major).

Experiment with this musical organization by finding the major template when you begin on any key. You don't have to know the exact key signature for each key. Just enjoy experimenting!

······· YELLOW ● LIGHT ·······

In popular- and jazz-style music, the pianist usually uses a lead sheet, which consists of a melody with chord symbols. The left hand part is not written out. The key signature in this type of music is written only on the first line, not on every line.

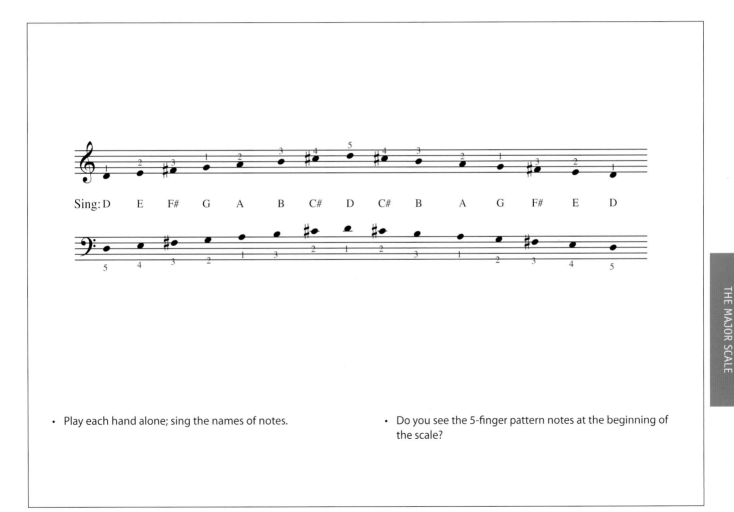

Sing: D E F# G A B C# D C# B A G F# E D

THE MAJOR SCALE

- Play each hand alone; sing the names of notes.

- Do you see the 5-finger pattern notes at the beginning of the scale?

101

SCALE DEGREES NUMBERED
Play a tune higher or lower by transposing

If you number the scale degrees, 1 through 7, you can substitute any scale for the one you are using. The sound is the same; the tune is either higher or lower.

Think about a very simple tune, "Mary Had a Little Lamb," and only the first phrase. It begins on the third note of the scale, and, according to the numbers, goes like this: 3-2-1-2-3-3-3. If you think or play it in the scale of C major, the notes are: E-D-C-D-E-E-E. You can move it higher, in the scale of D major, and it becomes: F#-E-D-E-F#-F#-F#. You can move it lower (or higher) to the scale of G major, and it becomes: B-A-G-A-B-B-B.

If you label every note with its step number in the scale, you can transpose it to another "key" by using those

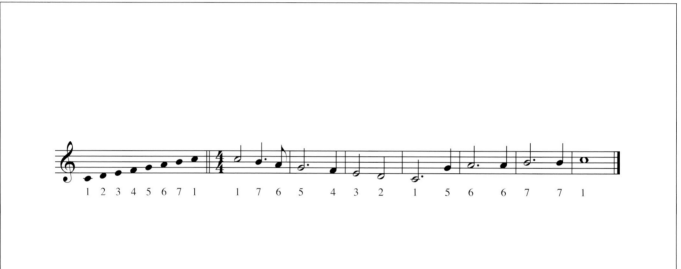

- Each note of the scale has a number.

- Wherever one particular note appears in the music, it has the same number.

- Look at the notation of the first two measures of "Joy to the World." Each note is numbered according to its place in scale.

- Now sing the song with the numbers.

- Play the tune starting on G.

numbers. The whole song, "Mary Had a Little Lamb," becomes, 3212333,222,355; 3212333322321. Sing it with these numbers. Play it in the key of C major. Now transpose it up to D major. It should sound the same. Since you used only the first five notes of the scale, you can play "Mary" in any of the five-finger patterns you are comfortable with.

In looking forward to chord labeling, start using Roman numerals to label the notes of the scale. Now you have I,II,III,IV,V,VI,VII,I.

YELLOW ● LIGHT

In music, always think from the lowest note up. When building chords, go up from the given note. When finding a scale pattern, always ascend from the starting note.

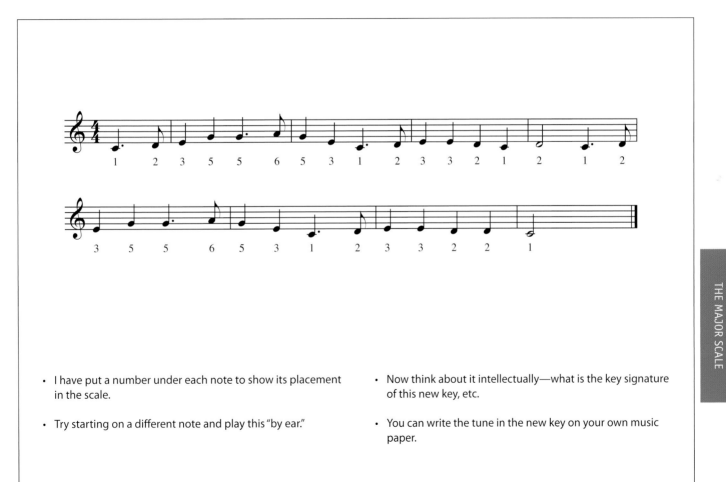

- I have put a number under each note to show its placement in the scale.

- Try starting on a different note and play this "by ear."

- Now think about it intellectually—what is the key signature of this new key, etc.

- You can write the tune in the new key on your own music paper.

THE MAJOR SCALE

THE MAGIC CIRCLE OF 5THS
You can see all the keys, all the key signatures, around this circle

Remember what the interval of a 5th is: from one letter name to another letter name, skipping three letter names. Play the note C, followed by the note G. The number of keys between them—black and white—is six. Now play B up to F; this is a 5th because the interval skips three letter names. But the sound is different. Count the keys between B and F; there are

only five! This 5th is not perfect (it's called "diminished"). To make it perfect you must play B up to F♯. Play both these 5ths, the perfect and the diminished, and listen to the difference in the sound.

To start you on your trip around the circle of 5ths, play the lowest C on your keyboard; up a perfect 5th is G. The scale

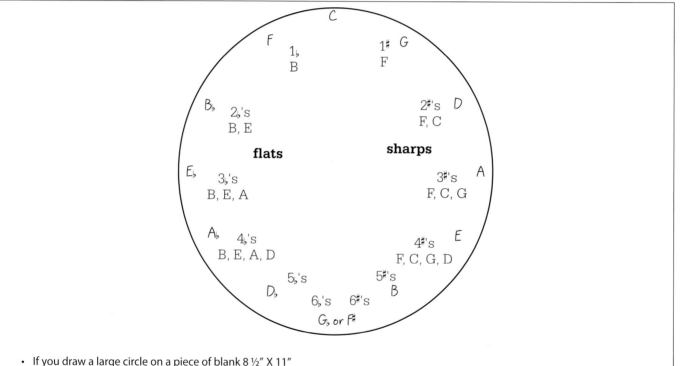

- If you draw a large circle on a piece of blank 8 ½" X 11" paper, you can draw and fill in your own circle of 5ths.

starting on G has one sharp. Go up a P5th from G, the note is D. The key of D major has two sharps. Go up a P5th from D, the note is A. Can you guess how many sharps there are? You can continue this way, discovering how the key signatures build up to seven sharps. By this time you have completed half the circle.

You have the name of the scale with all its keys sharped—C-sharp major—now continue around the circle by changing over to seven flats—C♭ major. A P5th up from C♭ is G♭.

This key has six flats. A P5th up from G♭ is D♭, which has five flats. Notice that you are now subtracting from the number of flats.

If you want the flat scales from one flat to seven flats, start at the top and go counter-clockwise, and DOWN the keyboard. Down a P5th from C is F—the key with one flat. Down a P5th from F is B♭—the key with two flats.

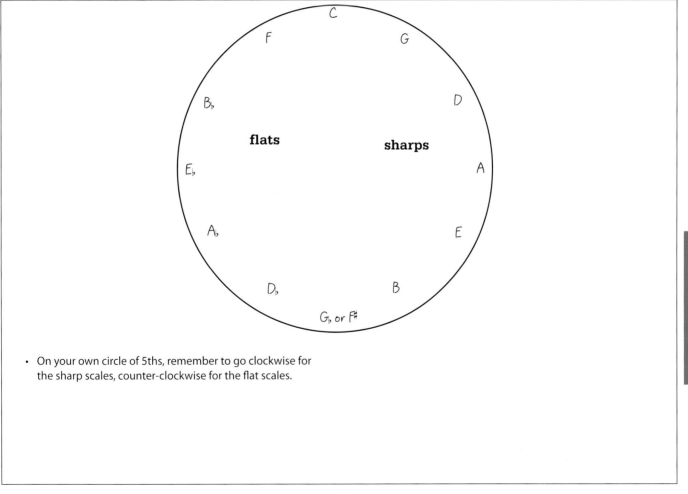

- On your own circle of 5ths, remember to go clockwise for the sharp scales, counter-clockwise for the flat scales.

MUSIC & QUESTIONS
Why? How? Ask the right questions and you can get the right answer

May I try to guess the questions you have?

1. Why is learning and practicing scales so important?

Because most of the music you enjoy is based on the major/minor system, and learning the scale and chord patterns gives you a head start in playing the music you hear and enjoy.

2. Why should I practice slowly, and how slow is "slow?"

You need to practice slowly because the brain has to be trained; play slowly so the brain does not learn mistakes (it is equally adept at learning something the wrong way!). You save time as well as effort.

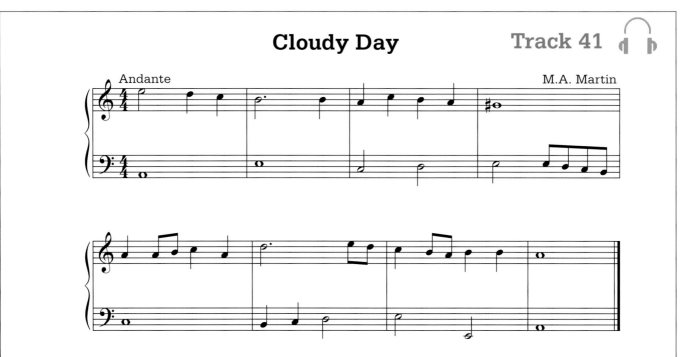

Cloudy Day
Track 41

Andante

M.A. Martin

• In your mind, go through the steps for learning a new piece: clap or tap the rhythm until it feels easy; look through the whole piece and choose logical fingering.

• Name the first note in each hand. Play each hand (if they play together) until it feels secure.

• Play hands together very slowly seven times. Then try it a little faster.

Purchase a metronome; or use the metronome on your keyboard. Set it to the lowest number (40 beats per minute on a non-digital one). That is slow! I find that when I warm up my fingers and hands with five-finger patterns, starting at 80 and letting the metronome tick two times per note keeps me slow enough.

3. Why don't the fingers of my left hand (or right hand) work properly?

The hand you do not write with, and sometimes the hand you do write with, has never had to do the small finger motions required for playing the piano. Patience! It may take weeks and months for you to feel comfortable playing the piano. As you slowly progress you need to recall that when you began you could not read a note of music, or play music. Appreciate each step of progress as it comes. Also, enjoy the process, and the way all of life's little problems (and sometimes big ones) seem to fade into the background, while you focus and concentrate on a new language that dictates the way your fingers move.

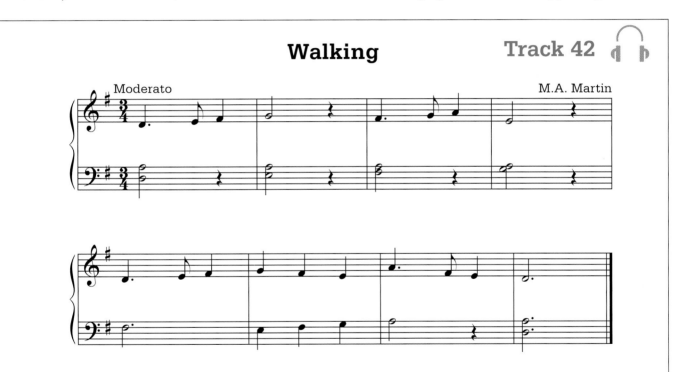

Walking

Track 42

Moderato

M.A. Martin

- Another piece in which to test your new skills. How long does it take to play the piece easily but slowly?

107

MUSIC TO ANALYZE
Try your hand (so to speak) at analyzing a piece of music

When you look at a piece of music, there is much to deduce about how it will sound before you play one note on the piano.

The title often tells you what kind of mood to set. If it is an abstract title, like Sonata, or Prelude, then look below the title on the left, just above the music. Whatever is written there should tell you what kind of mood to set. But it may be Italian words! A music dictionary will quickly divulge the meaning of the word(s).

The clef signs tell you the general area where you play, but be sure to look through the piece to the end. The clef signs can change!

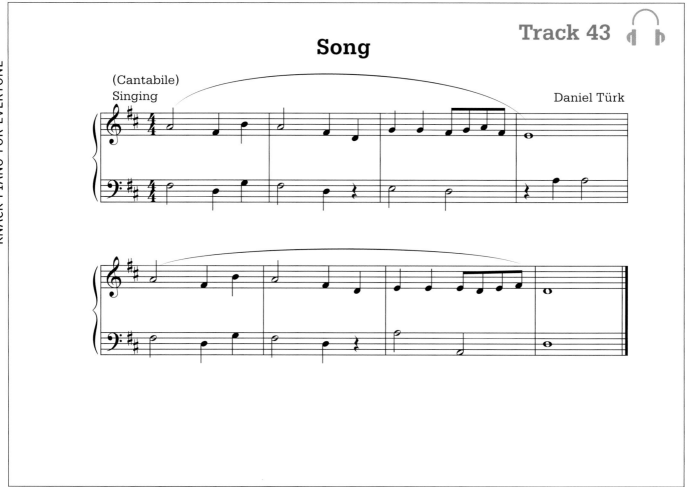

Track 43

Song

(Cantabile)
Singing

Daniel Türk

The key signature, which you discovered in the circle of 5ths, can tell you what the key is, and which notes/keys to sharp or flat. I like to play the scale of the piece I am practicing, so I can settle into the sound and finger patterns of the key.

The time signature tells not only how many beats are in a measure, but if the beat is divided into two notes or three notes (compound meter). Look at the first two measures and tap out the rhythm three or four times to get an idea of the sound.

Look for parts or measures that are alike or almost alike. Mark them so you know they will have the same or a similar sound.

If the piece is eight measures long or less, you can mark some finger numbers in by naming the direction and interval from one note to another.

If the piece is longer, divide it into sections, analyze each section and practice each section.

Track 44

Without a Care

(Allegro)
Cheerful

Daniel Türk

ORGANIZING PRACTICE TIME
Use your practice time wisely

I have learned over the years that I must get the most out of the short time I have to practice. I have to list my long-term and short-term goals, either in my head or on paper. If I have a choice of times, I must choose a time when my practicing does not disturb anyone else in the household, and a time when I am most alert.

It helps to practice at the same time of day, if that is possible.

Also, an electric keyboard with earphones makes it possible to practice just about anytime, anywhere.

There are many ways to organize your practice time. You may wish to keep a journal of your practices so you can log your accomplishments, and disappointments.

Go to a music store and explore their assignment books. One book may have an assignment page for each week, with

Organizers

WEEKLY LESSON PLAN

TODAY'S DATE:	
SCALES AND WARMUPS	SPECIFIC GOALS
ETUDES AND EXERCISES	SPECIFIC GOALS
REPERTOIRE	SPECIFIC GOALS
OTHER	SPECIFIC GOALS

- This organizer gives you a space to list pieces, and goals for each of the pieces for the week.

Space

WEEKLY LESSO

ETUDES AND EXERCISES	SPECIFIC GOALS
REPERTOIRE	SPECIFIC GOALS
OTHER	SPECIFIC GOALS

- This page gives you a space to list your accomplishments each day.

staff paper across from it for writing out scales, etc.

Another may be a real practice record, in which you may record the day's goals and progress, and the week's goals and progress. This gives you a perfect opportunity to reflect on your practice time and on your progress. It helps push you toward more complicated music and thinking.

············· RED ● LIGHT ·············

Like writers and composers, you need to work at your "art" every day. Some days your practice may seem completely worthless, and you may have felt you accomplished nothing; but often, the next day's practice will be wonderful and fulfilling. Every goal you made for yourself will have been accomplished!

Beautiful Dreamer

Stephen Foster

- Though you might know this tune, approach it like any other new piece: analyze and plan.

QUESTIONS

DYNAMIC VARIETY
The same sound coming from the piano all the time can become boring

Listen carefully to a recording of piano music. Whether it is new age or classical or jazz, the sound is changing constantly from soft, to loud, to very loud, to medium soft. These are called, "dynamics." The composer or arranger usually uses abbreviations for Italian words (yet again!) to mark the

dynamics: P for *piano* (soft), F for *forte* (loud), *mezzo*, used with P or F, for medium, PP for *pianissimo* (very soft) and FF for *fortissimo* (very loud).

   Often it is up to you, the piano player, to add dynamics (if not marked), or to vary the dynamics.

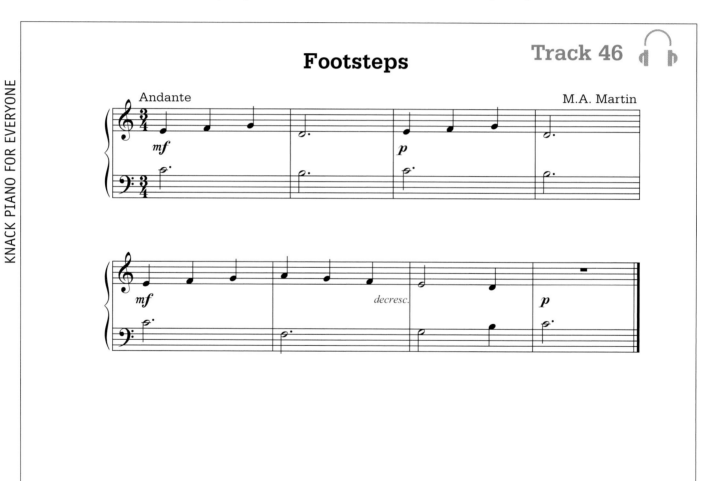

Footsteps

Track 46

Andante

M.A. Martin

When you are relaxed and in a comfortable playing position, you can get a "forte" sound by putting more weight behind the hands and fingers. Lean slightly toward the keyboard, and your shoulders and upper body add to the weight.

Less weight in the keys means a softer sound. But remember that the key must sink all the way into the keybed. You will have the feel of how deep the keybed is when you exercise each finger.

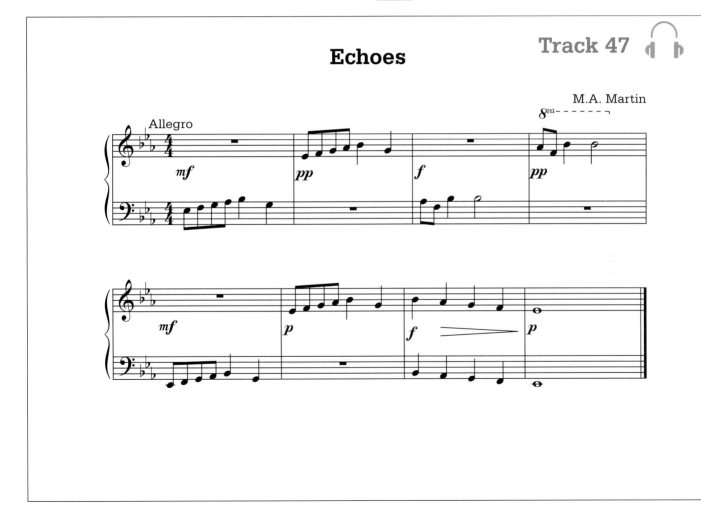

Echoes

Track 47

M.A. Martin

RITARDANDO, FERMATA, A TEMPO
Important directions to add variety to your tempo

Often in music, the abbreviation "rit" appears at the end of a section or at the end of the piece. This is the abbreviation for the word "*ritardando*," or "*ritenuto*," which means to gradually slow down.

If "rit" appears in the middle of a piece, it is sometimes followed by "a tempo," which means to return to the original tempo. Of course, the word tempo means time, or in our case, the beat—how fast or slow it is. When a whole section is marked slower than the original tempo, a return is marked "Tempo I."

Sometimes in the middle of a piece, a note has a fermata sign over it. Think of the end of the National Anthem, on the

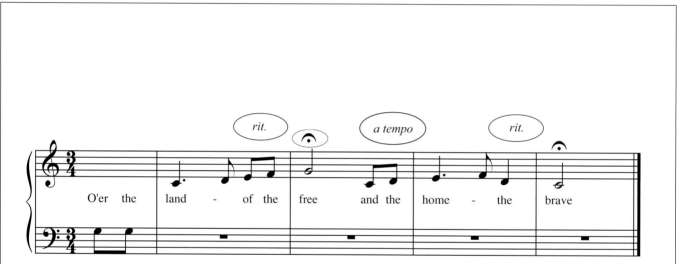

- All the tempo signs are circled for you to study.

phrase, "o'er the land of the free." The note with the word, "free" usually has a fermata sign over it; when we sing it, we hold the word "free" a little longer.

When there is a fermata, the beat stops, then continues "a tempo" (unless it is at the end of the piece). How long you hold the fermata note is dependent on what kind of note is held, how fast the tempo is, and your personal taste.

ZOOM

An opposite direction in the music is "accel.", short for *accelerando*, which obviously means to accelerate or go faster gradually. How much faster? That is a subjective decision. In fact, all these terms are left up to the performer, with advice from teachers, other performers, or friends.

Fiesta Time

traditional

- This is a more complicated piece, but I wanted you to see lots of signs.

QUESTIONS

MORE MUSIC
Pieces that use all, or most, of what you have learned so far

I have used some music from the eighteenth and nineteenth centuries, plus another song from Stephen Foster. Look at the slurs to help with parts, or sections. Study the intervals to help with finger numbers. Work out each hand carefully, by itself. Make sure each hand is easy before trying it hands together.

Slurs not only instruct you in seeing parts of a piece of music, they instruct you to play the notes under them smoothly and connected (legato). Think of singing a melody; where is it natural to breathe (I realize one may not be able to hold the breath for as long as a phrase!)?

Phrases in music are like phrases in a language. When you

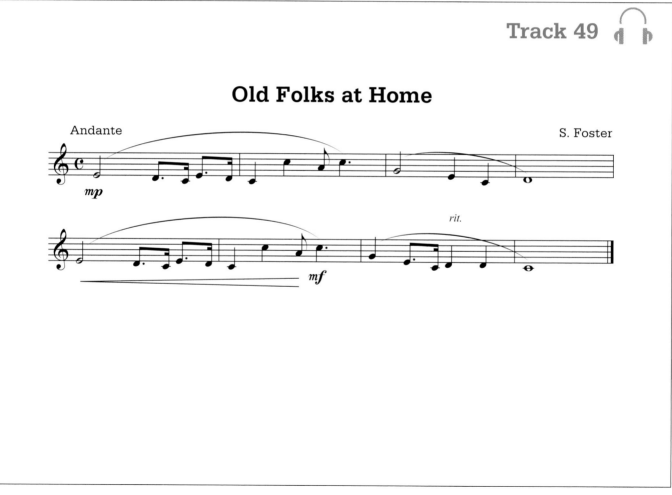

listen to a person talking, notice the rise and fall of the words, the emphasis on some words and not on others, the period at the end of a sentence. How do you finish a sentence? Does the voice rise, or does it go down to a softer tone? If the voice rises at the end, is it a question?

Listening to these variations will help you hear where the rise and fall of the phrases are. Good playing imitates the human voice, at its most eloquent, of course!

ZOOM

To help the performer, composers put different marks for extra stress. An accent (<) over or under a note means to give that note a little extra stress, but not a lot. *Sforzando (sFz),* or *forzando (Fz)* means more stress than the regular accent. Sometimes you may see "*subito piano.*" This means "suddenly quiet." *Crescendo* means to grow louder gradually. *Decrescendo* means to grow quieter gradually.

Track 50

page 117

D-FLAT MAJOR SCALE
Can you discover why this scale is similar to B major?

If you begin on D-flat and play up the scale (using the C major template) with one finger, you will discover that all five black keys are used, but are written as flats rather than sharps. That means that the scale of D-flat major will use the same fingering as B major: thumbs on the two white keys (F and C), 2-3 on the two black keys, 2,3,4 on the three black keys.

D-flat is enharmonic with, or is the same key as, C♯. In other words, they sound the same. The scale of C♯ (and the key of C♯) has seven sharps. When you can play the scale of D♭ major easily, you can play the scale of C♯ major easily also!

The three scales that use all five black keys (really six because of the enharmonic names) can be practiced the same way. What you have to remember is which two white keys the thumbs play. This is purely a topographical subject (I like to

Both Hands Play D-flat Major Scale

- The right hand has to prepare for the thumb to go under.

- Keep the right hand thumb gently tucked under finger 2 so that it is closer to the key it will play.

- Now play the thumbs in both hands and immediately prepare the three black keys.

- Left hand fingers 4-3-2 must cross over the thumb (think of a collapsed thumb) to prepare.

- Now the right hand thumb is playing the F key, and the left hand and arm have made an adjustment to help fingers 4,3,2 over the thumb.

- The wrist and arm form a straight line from the finger that is playing.

plan on which side of the black key to play the thumbs); but for help in reading music with five or six flats or sharps, name the notes of each scale, both ascending and descending. For C♯ and G♭, you can just remember that every note is sharp or every note is flat. For the keys of F♯ and G♭, you need to know which note is *not* sharp or flat. For B and D♭ major, the white keys are the natural keys. It makes sense that if C major has no sharps or flats, then C♯ major has every note sharp (seven sharps), and C♭ major has every note flat (seven flats). And C♭ is enharmonic with—you're correct—B!

- The fingers are playing the three black keys and the thumbs are on their next key, C.

- The right wrist and arm make an adjustment so that they form a straight line from elbow to thumb.

- You can practice this scale in small groups of notes, so that you are crossing over the thumb, then putting the thumb under, back and forth.

- Now you are back to a D-flat. The left hand and arm move slightly to accommodate finger 3 crossing over the thumb.

- You can play this scale for two octaves, up and down, in clusters, to feel relaxed and at ease.

- When you play the scale in single notes, play slowly and feel the depth of the keybed.

USING ALL FIVE BLACK KEYS
The topography of these scales helps make them easy to play

The third scale that uses all five black keys begins on F♯. Again, the thumbs will play the two white keys, B and E♯, 2-3 will play the two black keys, 2-3-4 will play the three black keys. When you can play the F♯ major scale easily, you can also play the enharmonic scale, G♭, major, easily.

F♯ major has six sharps; G♭ major has six flats. That means that one of the two white keys is a natural; it is not altered.

When you play the scale that begins on F♯/G♭, , think of the names of the keys you are playing. If you are playing the F♯ scale, the natural key is B; the other white key is E♯. If you are playing the G♭ scale, the natural key is F; the other white key is C♭.

Try this experiment: play any of the scales by starting on a different note in the scale. For example, begin the D♭ major

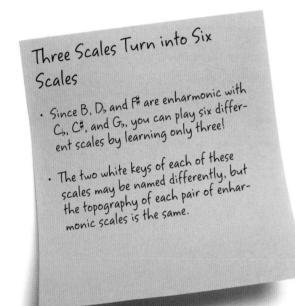

Three Scales Turn into Six Scales

- Since B, D♭, and F♯ are enharmonic with C♭, C♯, and G♭, you can play six different scales by learning only three!

- The two white keys of each of these scales may be named differently, but the topography of each pair of enharmonic scales is the same.

- Fingers 2-3-4, 4-3-2 are curved comfortably over the three black keys.

- RH finger 2 is leaving the F♯ as the thumb gets ready to play B.

- The left hand thumb is ready to play B, at which time the thumb will comfortably collapse so that fingers 3-2 can cross over the thumb.

scale on the F key. Play up one octave, to the next F, but play the D♭ scale notes. What is really different is the sound; you need to get used to this, and to hear the home key, D♭, as you play the D♭ major scale from F to F.

Continue to experiment starting on any other note of the scale, and playing up and down for one octave. Always keep the home key of the scale in your head.

Try playing one of the black key scales in contrary motion. These black key scales are rather easy to play hands together, since the finger groups, 2-3, and 2-3-4, and the thumbs, play at the same time. But in contrary motion you must play very slowly and think hard! Don't try this difficult exercise unless all the other ways of playing the scales are easy.

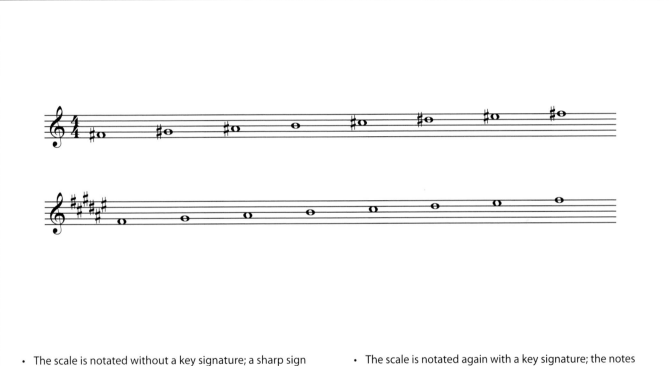

- The scale is notated without a key signature; a sharp sign has to go in front of each sharped note.

- The scale is notated again with a key signature; the notes are written without sharp signs, but you are expected to know which notes are sharped by looking at the key signature.

TECHNIQUE FOR WHITE KEY SCALES
Without black keys, it is difficult to plan the easiest fingering

Using the logical fingering of the "all black key" scales, we can devise a fingering for other scales. The right hand ascending finger scheme is 1, 2-3, 1, 2-3-4, 1, 2-3, 1, 2-3-4, 1.

The left hand ascending fingering scheme is 1, 4-3-2, 1, 3-2, 1, 4-3-2, 1, 3-2, 1. Depending on the scale, you can begin anywhere in these schemes.

When you start a scale in the left hand, and the second note requires finger 4, you may use finger 5. Likewise, in the right hand, if the next to the last note at the top of the scale is played by finger 4, you may use finger 5 on the last note.

In music, you rarely see a scale that starts and ends on its "tonic," or home key. To help you get to know each scale better, start on a different note of the scale and play up and down an octave. In the E major scale, for example, start and

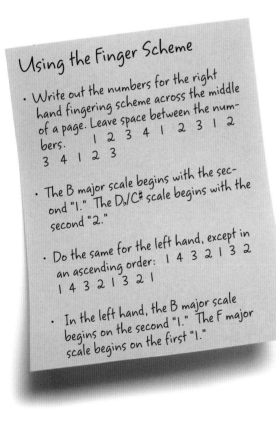

Using the Finger Scheme
• Write out the numbers for the right hand fingering scheme across the middle of a page. Leave space between the numbers. 1 2 3 4 1 2 3 1 2 3 4 1 2 3
• The B major scale begins with the second "1." The D♭/C# scale begins with the second "2."
• Do the same for the left hand, except in an ascending order: 1 4 3 2 1 3 2 1 4 3 2 1 3 2 1
• In the left hand, the B major scale begins on the second "1." The F major scale begins on the first "1."

Playing the E Major Scale

- By playing a major scale with one finger, you discover that the E major scale has four black keys.

- Because of the dictum that says "seven different letter names," you can see that the black keys are sharps—there are four sharps in the key of E major.

- There is a white key, then two black keys, followed by two white keys, then two black keys. This dictates that the RH should start with finger 1, then 2-3, then 1.

end on F#. At the next practice, perhaps the next day, start and end the E major scale on G#. We are so accustomed to singing, "Do, re, mi," etc. that we rarely listen for the relationship of the keys when starting in a different place.

Don't forget the other hand!

Climbing Up, Sliding Down

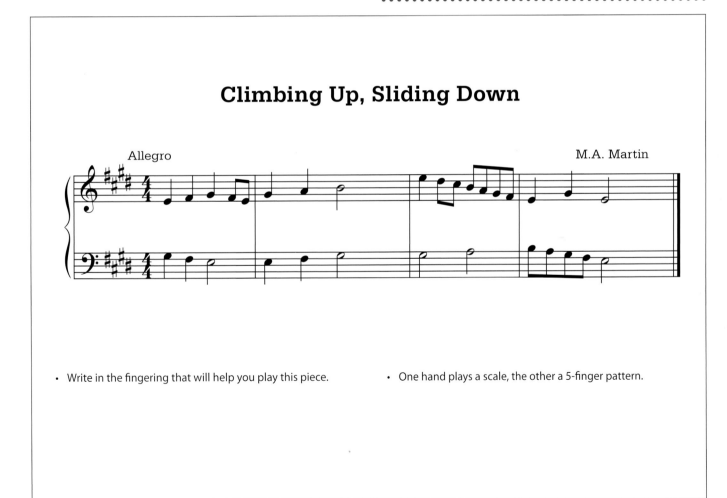

Allegro   M.A. Martin

- Write in the fingering that will help you play this piece.

- One hand plays a scale, the other a 5-finger pattern.

C MAJOR/CONTRARY MOTION
Since there are no black keys, any fingering will do!

It helps our playing if there is some consistency. So let's play the C major scale, right hand, like the B major scale ascending. We can also use that fingering, 1-2-3-1-2-3-4-5, for the left hand, descending the C major scale. Play this scale hands together, both thumbs starting on middle C, going in opposite directions—right hand up, left hand down. The finger numbers are the same, and there are no black keys. You can

play for one octave, end on fifth fingers, and come right back. Playing in opposite directions is called "contrary motion."

When you play other scales in contrary motion, think and play carefully. Even if the finger numbers are the same, different fingers will fall on black keys. Make sure each hand can play the scale up and down easily before attempting hands together either in contrary motion or parallel motion.

C Major Scale in Contrary Motion

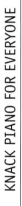

- Both hands have their thumbs on middle C.

- You may think they don't fit, but you are only playing the sides of the tips of the thumbs.

- If your thumbs truly don't fit on one key, let one thumb

play it while the other thumb hovers, ready to play finger 2.

- Remember to elevate the hands slightly so the thumbs can pass under fingers two and three easily.

- Both thumbs are passing under the third fingers.

- Both hands are slightly elevated to make this easy.

- The wrists and arms make a slight adjustment to allow weight behind the fingers that are playing.

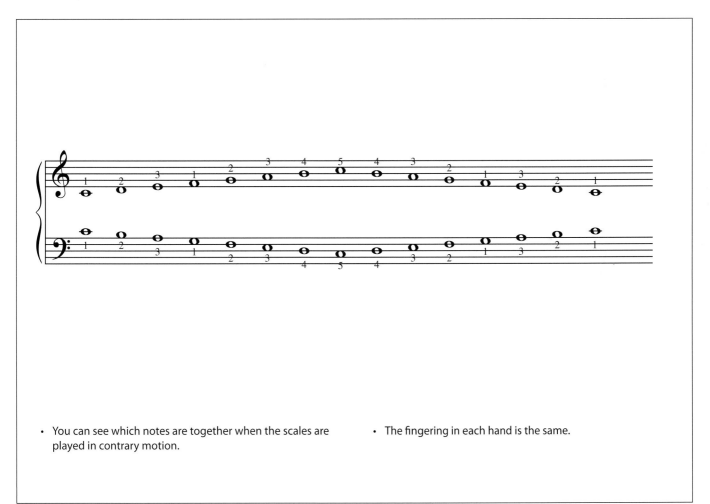
When you play the scale hands together, go slowly. Count two to each note so you can think about which key to play, whether it is a black key or white key, which finger plays it. Since both hands want to do the same action, you have to persuade the other hand to move differently.

Now that you have played the C major scale in contrary motion slowly, try speeding up gradually. Use a metronome to gauge the progress. Start at 72, one tick per note, and move it up two notches for the second time, another two

notches for the third time. Now turn off the metronome and play the scale fast.

If eight-note scales are difficult in contrary motion, try playing your old friends, the five-finger patterns, in contrary motion. F major will be the easiest (I'm not even considering the twins!), followed by E major, then the gnarly B major. When you can play these easily, change them to minor five-finger patterns.

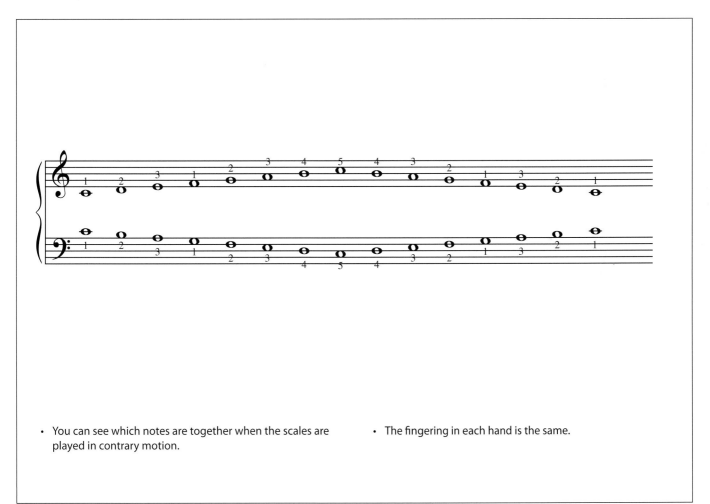

- You can see which notes are together when the scales are played in contrary motion.

- The fingering in each hand is the same.

TOPOGRAPHY OF SCALES
You can figure out fingerings for all scales, one hand at a time

In fingering a scale, the thumb should not play a black key. I'm not saying that the thumb should never play a black key; but to play a scale passage in music smoothly and evenly, with a controlled touch, it is easier if the thumbs play white keys.

As you find the easiest fingering for each scale, be sure to have the hands play separately. Many scales are not conducive to playing hands together until each hand is comfortable with the pattern.

When you go around the circle of 5ths counter-clockwise, you start at C then go down a 5th. That is the note F, which begins the next scale. It will have one flat. The left hand fingering for this scale, going up, is the same as C major: 5-4-3-2-1-3-2-1. The right hand will have to finger 1-2-3-4, because

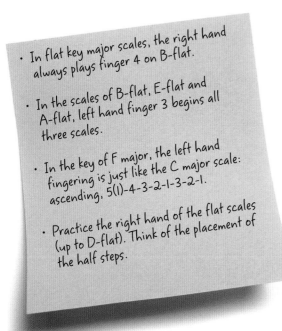

- In flat key major scales, the right hand always plays finger 4 on B-flat.

- In the scales of B-flat, E-flat and A-flat, left hand finger 3 begins all three scales.

- In the key of F major, the left hand fingering is just like the C major scale: ascending, 5(1)-4-3-2-1-3-2-1.

- Practice the right hand of the flat scales (up to D-flat). Think of the placement of the half steps.

A-Flat Major: Both Hands

- Left hand fingers 3-2, right hand fingers 3-4 are prepared on their keys.

- Both thumbs will play the white key, C.

- When the thumbs play C, the left hand fingers 4-3 immediately cross over the thumb to play D♭. But watch out! The second finger will play a white key.

of the B♭, then play 1-2-3 and end with finger 4 on F if playing only one octave.

Continuing around the circle of 5ths, go down a perfect 5th from F to B♭. That is the name of the new key, which has two flats, and the name of the starting note. Since the right hand usually plays finger 4 on B♭, the starting finger of the right hand is finger 4, followed by 1-2-3, 1-2-3-4. The left hand begins on finger 3-2-1, 4-3-2-1-3.

E♭ major, with three flats, begins with left hand finger 3, and goes on to fingers 2-1-4-3-2-1-3. The right hand starts with finger 3, followed by 1-2-3-4-1-2-3.

Have you noticed as you moved around the circle that new flats (and sharps, going clockwise) are just added on to the flats (and sharps) already there? The order of the flats, whether there are two or seven, always begins with B♭. The order of flats spells a word for the first four letters: B, E, A, D.

Waltz in A♭ Major

Allegro

M.A. Martin

CIRCLE OF 5THS, AGAIN
Finish the other half of the circle, with the flat keys

Start at the top of the circle, and the top of the piano keyboard, and go down a P5th, counterclockwise on the circle. F is the key you rest on. The key of F major has one flat; play every white key from F up to the next F with one finger. There is one note that sounds out of place; that note is B. Play B♭ instead, and you have the F major scale, with a key signature of one flat.

Continuing down the keyboard a P5th, the next note is B♭. Play the keys from B♭ through all white keys, up to the next B♭. The note that sounded out of place is E. Between your ear and your knowledge of the scale pattern, you will flat the E. The new flat is the fourth note of the scale.

As you journey through the flat keys you will discover all sorts

KNACK PIANO FOR EVERYONE

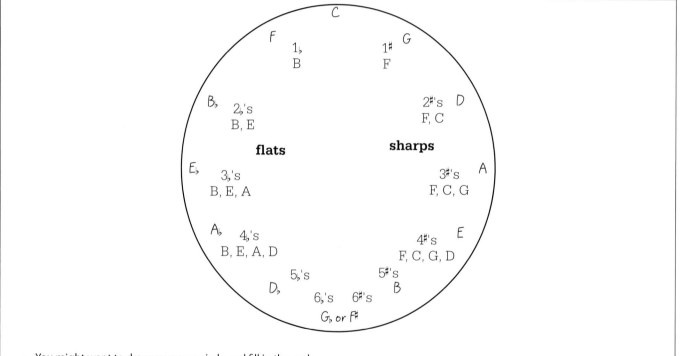

- You might want to draw your own circle and fill in the scale names and the number of sharps or flats.

128

of coincidences. The new flat of each key, as you go around the circle counter-clockwise, is the fourth note of the scale. The new flat becomes the name of the next key in the circle. In the scale of F, B♭, was the new flat. That became the home key of the next scale, and so forth around the left side of the circle.

If you go around the sharp side again, starting at the top, you will find that the new sharp in each scale is the seventh note of the scale. Therefore, you can name the scale right away if you know the last sharp and go up a half step.

YELLOW LIGHT

The key signature has been mentioned as a time saver; rather than sharp or flat each note as it comes, just write the sharps or flats that you will use all the time at the beginning of each line. You don't need to memorize the order of sharps and flats, but you should understand how it relates to the circle of 5ths.

MORE SCALES

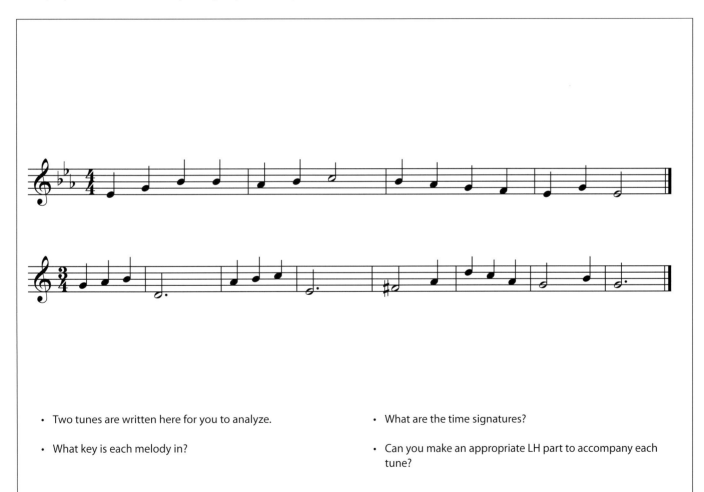

- Two tunes are written here for you to analyze.

- What key is each melody in?

- What are the time signatures?

- Can you make an appropriate LH part to accompany each tune?

THE FAMILY OF KEYS
Just like cousins, major and minor keys have something in common

Major scales have minor scales that are relatives—they share the same key signature. We call them "relative minor scales." The default "template" is A to A, all white keys. The pattern for this "natural" minor is: half steps between degrees 2 and 3, 5 and 6. All other steps are whole steps. You can say, "A minor is relative to C major."

You can take different approaches to finding and playing minor scales. The first way is to take the template pattern described above and start on any key.

The second way is to find the note in the major scale that begins the minor scale, and simply play the major scale beginning and ending on a different note.

Move around the circle of 5ths to G major. The sixth note of the G major scale is E; it is also located three half steps below

C Major and A Minor scales

- The major scale has dots on the keys.

- The minor scale has asterisks on the keys. Half steps are marked.

- Play up and down both scales to hear their relationship.

- Using the same relationship, try to find relative minor keys for G major and F major.

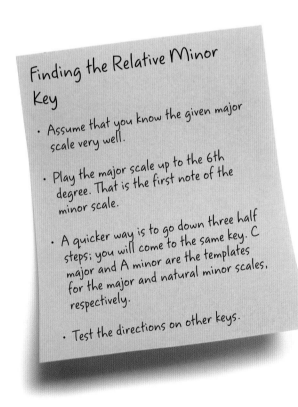

Finding the Relative Minor Key

- Assume that you know the given major scale very well.

- Play the major scale up to the 6th degree. That is the first note of the minor scale.

- A quicker way is to go down three half steps; you will come to the same key. C major and A minor are the templates for the major and natural minor scales, respectively.

- Test the directions on other keys.

G. Play a scale from E to the next E, using white keys except for F, which becomes F♯ in this key. Play it again and think of the steps between the keys: whole step from E to F♯, half step from F♯ to G, then whole step, whole step, half step, whole step, whole step to the next E. You have just played the E natural minor scale. When a piece of music is in the key of E minor, the home key is E, and there is one sharp in the key signature: F♯.

If you have drawn a circle of 5ths, you can start filling in the relative minor keys beside the major keys for each key signature. As part of your warm-up routine, play a major scale followed by its relative minor. Use whatever fingering comes natural to you, but plan to keep your thumbs on white keys.

- You can see how closely related these two scales are.

- Many classical period (app.1750–1850) sonatas, symphonies, and string quartets use key changes that go from the minor to its relative major.

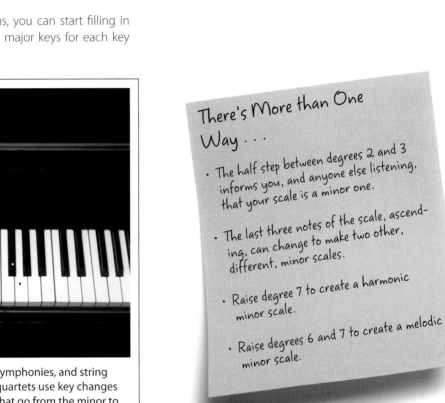

There's More than One Way . . .

- The half step between degrees 2 and 3 informs you, and anyone else listening, that your scale is a minor one.

- The last three notes of the scale, ascending, can change to make two other, different, minor scales.

- Raise degree 7 to create a harmonic minor scale.

- Raise degrees 6 and 7 to create a melodic minor scale.

HARMONIC MINOR
This scale reminds me of a snake charmer

When you play the harmonic minor scale, you can picture exotic places, or remember stories about Ali Baba or Sinbad the Sailor. The harmonic minor is sometimes called the Mohammedan scale because it sounds like a common mode in Arabic music. But there is the technical proponent; when you raise the 7th degree, you make a step and a half between degrees six and seven. This is not much of a problem in the left hand in A minor, since the step and a half is between fingers three and two; but in the right hand the step and a half is between fingers three and four. You will need to practice playing these two notes back and forth. Move the forearm slightly with finger three and finger four, so that each finger has support.

RH Plays Step and a Half

- The space between fingers 3 and 4 has to be stretched to reach the G♯.

- Play back and forth on these keys, moving the arm slightly with the finger so there is support.

- Add the 5th finger to your exercise and play back and forth.

- If you continue up the scale you need to play finger 1 after the 4th finger, so play that pattern slowly several times, keeping the arm and wrist aligned with whichever finger is playing.

LH Plays Step and a Half

- The stretch from finger 1 on F to finger 4 on A♯ is much easier.

- Practice this interval with the thumb playing C, then passing under 3 (down) to play G.

- Go back and forth, feeling loose in the arm and wrist.

- Now practice playing on up from C, to B with finger 4. Again, go back and forth, keeping the arm and wrist aligned with the finger that is playing.

Listen for this harmonic minor scale in Mozart's Symphony no. 40 in G minor. He states the opening theme starting with a half step repeated three times ending with the interval of a sixth going up; then he descends through a natural minor scale, stopping on C. He then repeats the opening theme one note lower (it's a whole step this time), goes up a sixth, and descends the G harmonic minor scale, beginning on the note A, and ending on the note B♭.

For those on the opposite end of the musical spectrum,

heavy metal music often employs the harmonic minor scale. There are thousands of examples of minor music, and many of those use the harmonic minor, but not many use the scale format of the harmonic minor.

A Minor Scale on the Staff

- Play the scale slowly in each hand.

- Play it hands together; count 2 to each note.

- Transpose the harmonic scale to E minor.

- Try other minor scales, playing natural minor first, then raising the 7th degree to make it harmonic.

MELODIC MINOR
For some the step and a half is an awkward sound

The awkwardness of the harmonic minor scale is not only technical. Singing the step and a half interval is also awkward. In melodic music, you will find the awkward interval negated by also raising the sixth degree. In the scale, we usually play up the melodic minor by raising degrees 6 and 7, then descending the natural minor, or flatting (lowering) degrees 7 and 6. But, you can find exceptions.

Examples of melodic and natural minor scales can be found in Mozart's Piano Sonata in A major, K. 331. The first movement is a theme and variations plan. Variation no. 3 is in A minor. Even though Mozart uses several G sharps throughout the variation, he manages to avoid the step from F to G# by using the melodic minor form of the scale.

In the third movement, labeled "alla Turca," Mozart uses the

RH Plays Melodic Minor

- The right hand is playing the more finger-friendly melodic minor scale.

- Fingers 2-3-4 are on E, F♯ and G♯. You can play finger 5 on the next A, or finger 1 if you are continuing up the scale.

- If you play finger 5 on A, play the descending scale, which will be G natural, F natural, E, etc. It feels a little different and should be practiced until it feels easy.

LH Plays Melodic Minor

- Left hand finger 3 is crossing over the thumb to play F♯, finger 2 to play G♯. Continue on to A with the thumb.

- Practice going down the scale (changed to natural minor) playing finger 2 on G, finger 3 on F, then thumb under to play E.

- Go back and forth on this pattern at the top of the scale, making sure thumb, arm, and wrist are always relaxed.

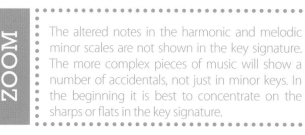

key of F# minor beginning in measure no. 33. Again, he avoids the awkward step and a half by using melodic minor patterns.

Since the melodic scale change to natural occurs often, in some form or another, practice the last four notes of the scale going up, then descending the scale in the natural form. Don't repeat the top note, but play, E-F#-G#-A-G-F-E, in the right hand five times, and in the left hand five times.

Practice the ascending and descending pattern in several different keys.

ZOOM

The altered notes in the harmonic and melodic minor scales are not shown in the key signature. The more complex pieces of music will show a number of accidentals, not just in minor keys. In the beginning it is best to concentrate on the sharps or flats in the key signature.

MINOR SCALES

Melodic Minor Scale on Grand Staff

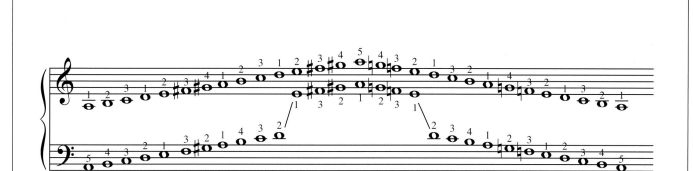

RELATING MINOR TO MAJOR

Many compositions illustrate the strong family ties between minor keys and their relative majors

Mozart's 40th Symphony, first movement, is a good example of a minor key and its relative major. The opening theme is in G minor, eight plus ten measures; then he repeats the theme, but ends it in B♭ major. It is a beautiful segue from minor to relative major. The second phrase of four measures is a harmonic scale descending.

Have some fun by practicing the G minor harmonic scale, up and down, with whichever hand you are most comfortable. Then practice the B♭ major scale. Locate degree V of the G minor scale, then degree V of the B♭ major scale. Now

Track 57

Mozart's Symphony No. 40 in G minor, 1st movement

- Here is a melody using both minor and major keys. Can you find the relation?

play a recording of Mozart's 40th Symphony and try playing along. It doesn't hurt anyone, and it can be entertaining and engrossing!

Try playing along with other recordings. I don't mean to play every note; just try different notes on the piano and find just one that fits. Then find another. When the song or piece ends, try finding the ending note.

Another example of minor going to its relative major is, "In the Hall of the Mountain King," by Grieg. (This piece is about trolls having a good old time!) It begins with that familiar minor sound, going up the minor five-finger pattern; then the melody repeats but slides easily into the relative major key. Then the whole theme repeats exactly.

Make a chart of the major keys and their relative minors and review it until they become second nature: F major and D minor; G major and E minor; A major and F♯ minor; and so on.

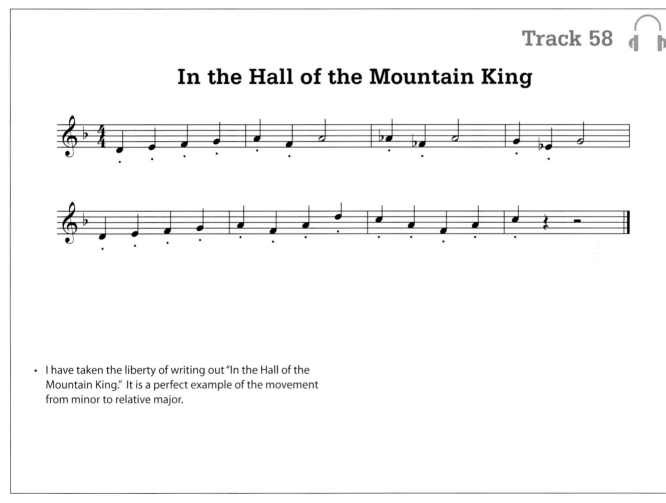

Track 58

In the Hall of the Mountain King

- I have taken the liberty of writing out "In the Hall of the Mountain King." It is a perfect example of the movement from minor to relative major.

MUSIC WITH MINOR SOUND
Think about all the Halloween music, horror movie music, and suspenseful music

We can begin listing pieces in minor keys and fill up these pages quickly! If a movie needs to be portrayed as scary, or strange, minor key music does the trick! What immediately comes to mind is Hedwig's theme in the *Harry Potter* movies.

At the opposite end of the spectrum, the opening theme of "Stairway to Heaven" is in a natural minor key; but it doesn't seem scary. Grieg's "Peer Gynt Suite" has several pieces in minor—Ase's Death, which is just sad; Anitra's Dance, which sounds lively and happy, and the very familiar "In the Hall of the Mountain King," which is lively in a humorous way and

Track 59

Country Dance Tunes

- Here are some tunes for you to play and listen to.

- Experiment with a Left hand accompaniment, perhaps blocked 5ths or single notes.

- Play these with the right hand; then play an octave or two lower with the left hand.

ends very wildly. (This last piece is another example of music moving from minor to the relative major by the end of the first eight measures.)

So you don't have to connect minor to sadness, or tragedy, or feeling scared. But if you want to project those moods, minor is definitely your key.

Broadway musicals have some wonderful examples of major and minor keys. For minor, think of "Sunrise, Sunset" from *Fiddler on the Roof*. For a rather sad major key, think of "Edelweiss" from *The Sound of Music*. Now that you have your thinking cap on, I bet you can come up with dozens of tunes that are obviously minor, or obviously major. Make a list!

Beethoven's Fifth Symphony is in C minor. The last movement of this four-movement opus is in C major. This is related to C minor only because the "home" key of both is C. But the key signatures are very different. Musicians call this the "parallel" minor.

- "Marche Slav" is written out for you to practice. It is in a minor-sounding key, but the step and a half interval comes between degrees 3 and 4.

- When you have mastered the melody, try adding the simple left hand accompaniment, or make up your own accompaniment!

MORE MUSIC
You can have some fun playing these minor key tunes

If you have your circle of 5ths, go around the circle and write in the relative minor keys with each major key. Of course they will be a 5th apart also. Decide which of the major scales you play the best and play the relative minor scales of those keys. Give each hand a chance to do this.

Get to know your scales/keys even better by playing each scale in 3rds. Start in C major; with right hand, play fingers 4-2 together on C and E. Ascend the scale in this "double 3rd" fashion. Finger 2 is playing the usual scale notes, finger 4 is playing a 3rd above. This is easy! Be sure to let the left hand have a go at this new way of playing a scale.

Now try this in other keys; G major and F major are the

Track 61

"Dance of the Sugar Plum Fairy"
from The Nutcracker

P. Tchaikovsky, arr. M.A. Martin

KNACK PIANO FOR EVERYONE

obvious choices. You have to think carefully because both fingers have to play the correct black keys. Again, left hand gets equal time.

It's time to try this scale in 3rds in a minor key. This is getting more interesting! A minor, natural is no problem, but the harmonic and melodic scales take a little thinking.

Below I have chosen some classical music for you to analyze and practice.

Study each melody to decide which minor key it belongs to. Go back to the circle of 5ths and find the relative major key. Can you transpose each melody to another minor key?

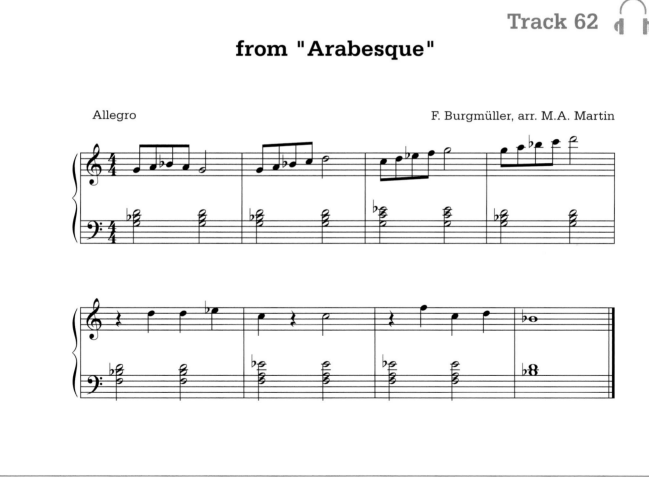

Track 62

from "Arabesque"

Allegro

F. Burgmüller, arr. M.A. Martin

TRIADS ON EVERY NOTE

Play a triad on every note of the major scale, staying in the key

C major is once again our "default" key. Triads built on every note of the scale will involve only white keys. Play each of these chords and listen to the quality of the sound. Some will be major, some will be minor. The triad built on degree VII sounds strange—not major, not minor. It is called "diminished." The different qualities of these chords come from the intervals that separate the notes.

You already know the difference between a perfect 5th and a diminished 5th (smaller by a half step). There are two kinds of 3rds—major and minor. Obviously, the minor 3rd is smaller than the major 3rd, by a half step. Compare the notes C up to E (count the keys in between them), then C up to E♭. The first interval is a major 3rd; the second interval is a minor 3rd. Play them each again, blocked, then broken. Close your eyes and

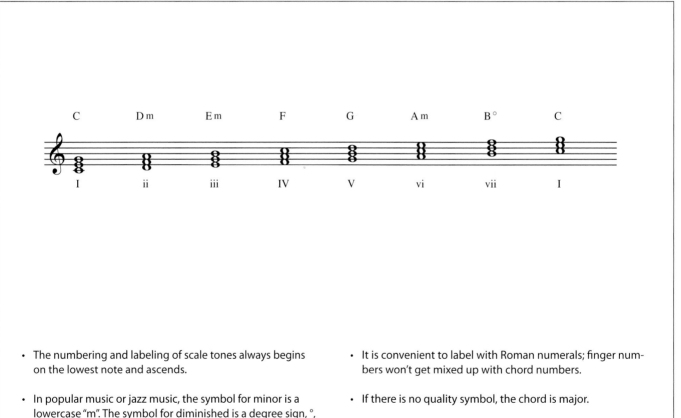

- The numbering and labeling of scale tones always begins on the lowest note and ascends.

- In popular music or jazz music, the symbol for minor is a lowercase "m". The symbol for diminished is a degree sign, °, or a lower case "d."

- It is convenient to label with Roman numerals; finger numbers won't get mixed up with chord numbers.

- If there is no quality symbol, the chord is major.

hear the difference in the sound.

If you examine the C major triad closely, you will find that the outside 5th—C up to G—is perfect. The interval of a 3rd—from C up to E—is a major one (count the keys between the two notes). From E up to G is a minor 3rd (count the keys between the two notes).

Now you know what a major triad consists of. Find other major triads and test out these qualities.

Now play once again the triads built on each note of the C major scale. Listen for the major triads, the minor triads, and

that strange-sounding triad built on B—the diminished triad. It is made of two minor 3rds. The outside 5th is diminished.

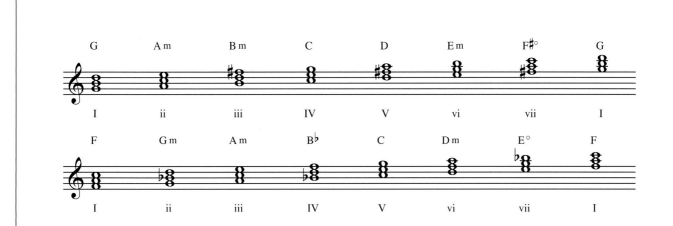

- As you play every chord in the scale, you discover that there are only three major chords.

- All the other chords are minor, except VII, which is diminished.

OTHER KEYS, OTHER TRIADS
Get to know the keys by building chords on every note of the scale

For some in-depth practice of a key, build chords on every note of the scale, but stay in the key. In other words, when playing chords in the key of G major, any chord with an F has to use the note F♯. Be sure to give the other hand the same opportunity!

You will also find that the quality of each chord is the same as the corresponding triad in C major.

This is great practice for getting to know your keys! Play in the keys of one and two sharps and flats, triads on each key. You have to think hard, but get accustomed to the "language" of each new key.

You can now start labeling the chords with Roman numerals: I, II, III, IV, V, VI, VII, I. Circle the chords that sound like major. They should be the same in each key. Put small "m's" under

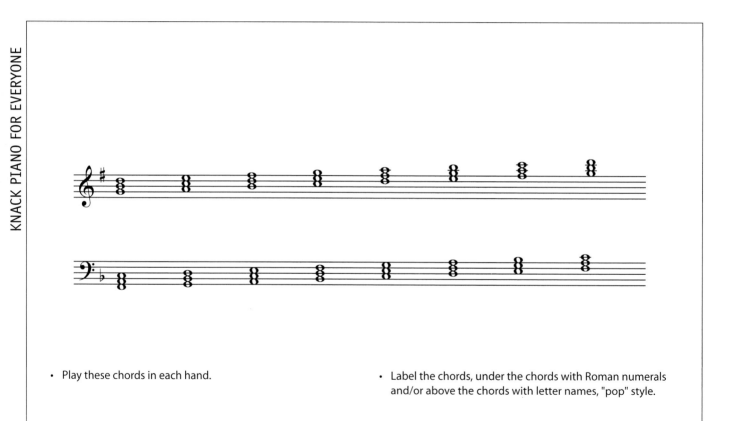

• Play these chords in each hand.

• Label the chords, under the chords with Roman numerals and/or above the chords with letter names, "pop" style.

the minor chords, a small "d" under the diminished chord.

This theory of chords (harmony), with the bass or "root" tones relating to each other in a musical way, was penned by Jean-Philippe Rameau in 1722. We are still using this harmonic organization! There are other digressions and other theories composers use, but for all of us, this basic harmonic theory is important and useful.

BUILDING CHORDS

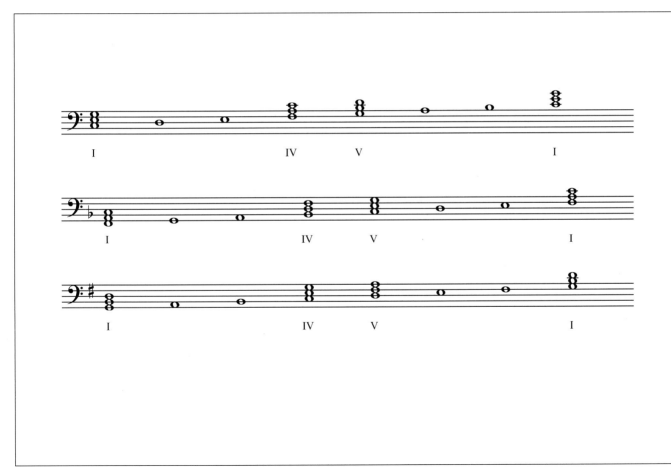

PRIMARY CHORDS

In building chords on every scale note, you will discover only three major ones

As you play chords on every note of the C major scale, listen for the quality of each chord. Choose the three major chords—C, F, and G major—and play them several times. These are the "primary chords." Play them broken, then blocked. You are getting used to moving from chord to chord.

Test the interval structure of each chord: Is the 5th perfect?

Is the major 3rd the lower interval, minor 3rd the upper interval?

You can accompany just about any tune with these three chords, and sometimes you only need I and V, or just I.

The list of three-chord songs is endless! Typical are the tunes "Oh, When the Saints," "This Land is Your Land," "Michael

Left Hand on C Major Chord

- The arm is parallel to the floor.
- The palm of the hand has a nice "dome."
- Thumb is on its side and slanted toward the wrist.
- The fifth finger is tall, not collapsed.

Left Hand on F Major Chord

- The hand looks the same as it did on the C major chord.
- Since the pressed keys are all white, the fingers are slightly away from the black keys.

Row the Boat Ashore," and "Yellow Submarine."

Usually at the end of these tunes the chord progression V to I is used. This is the sound that gives such finality to a piece. It is called a "cadence." Often the interval of a 7th is added to the penultimate chord to make that chord more dissonant and to make the progression toward the end more active. Play, in the key of C major, the V or G chord and add one more third on the top. This will read G-B-D-F; the interval from the root note, G, to the top note, F, is a 7th. Play this seventh chord, labeled V7 or G7, with two hands (two notes in each hand). Then play the I or C chord. Listen to some Beethoven symphonies and overtures. Beethoven often used the V to I cadence for dramatic effect. At the end of the Fifth Symphony he repeats the progression V to I many times. You can play the keys G to C along with the recording. Can you tell if he uses the seventh of the G chord?

Left Hand on G Major Chord

- The hand looks the same, in a strong, controlled, relaxed position.

- Practice moving between these three chords: C, F, to G.

- Change the order: C to G to F to G to C. Play these blocked, then broken.

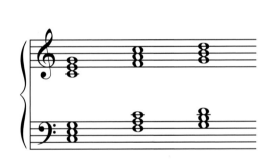

- Here are the primary chords written on the staff, in both the treble and the bass.

- Play the chords adding a C chord at the end.

- Count evenly, 2 or 3 beats per chord.

147

"LA BAMBA"

A familiar tune, with only primary chords for accompaniment

"La Bamba" is a traditional Latin melody. You need only the three primary chords to accompany the tune. Play the C major chord, to the F major chord, to the G major chord. Hold the G major chord twice as long as the other two. If you do this over and over, you have played accompaniment for the whole song! The melody begins on (up an octave, away from the left hand), and there are not many different notes.

If you play the primary chords in a broken style, left hand fingers 5-3-1, 5-3-1, 5-3-1, you can make a more interesting accompaniment. Try it in the other hand also. (In the right hand the finger numbers will be 1-3-5.)

Make up the simplest tune possible by playing the chords in one hand, and one note of the chord in the other hand. In the key of C major, the very simple melody will be C, F, G.

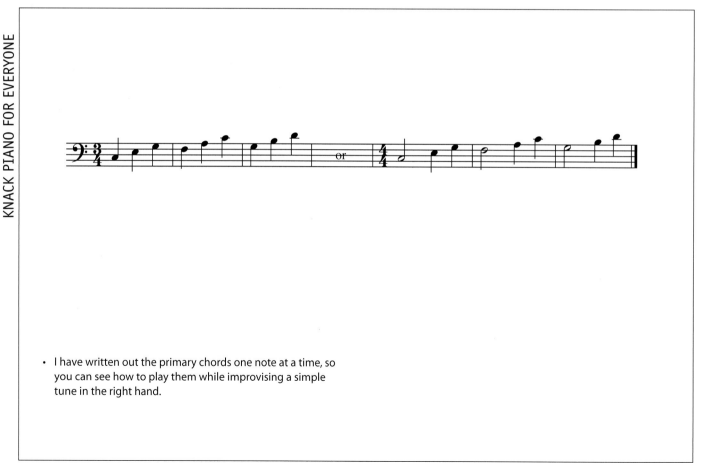

- I have written out the primary chords one note at a time, so you can see how to play them while improvising a simple tune in the right hand.

Now try the middle note of each chord in the other hand: the melody will be E, A, B. This very simple way of improvising should give you a boost toward making up your own melody.

To make it easier to improvise, hold each left hand chord down for four long beats. This will give you time to play the notes of the chord one at a time in the right hand, and play some notes in between. If you play the C major five-finger pattern, you are playing the triad with passing notes in between.

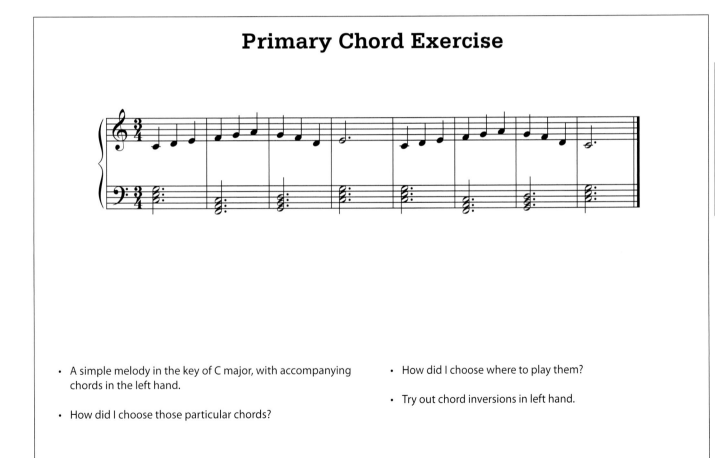

Primary Chord Exercise

- A simple melody in the key of C major, with accompanying chords in the left hand.

- How did I choose those particular chords?

- How did I choose where to play them?

- Try out chord inversions in left hand.

ADD SYNCOPATION
This is beginning to sound almost like "salsa" music!

The word "syncopation" means to move a strong beat over to a weaker beat. This music is more difficult to read, because it takes more notation to write it correctly. As in other rhythmic patterns, you need to feel it first. Listen to Latin-based popular music—it is all syncopated. The main beats are either anticipated or delayed. Jazz and rock and roll music are also performed this way. Listen to a popular song, then look at

the music for it. It usually looks very complicated, unless you have the simplest arrangement.

A good example of this is "Linus and Lucy" from the *Peanuts* cartoons. If you try to play the melody by ear, you will find that the first section consists of only three notes, whole steps apart. But look at the printed music and listen to a recording. The syncopations sound normal and easy to play; but a

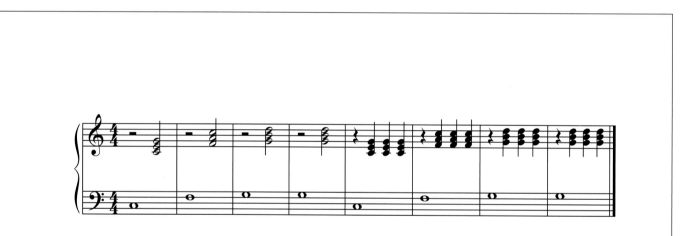

- Another way to accompany a simple tune like "La Bamba" is to play the bass note, or name-of-the-chord note, in the left hand, the chord in the right hand.

- You want to make it fit into four measures of 4/4 time.

glance at the music tells you it is not as easy as you thought, at least hands together.

"The Girl from Ipanema" is another example of a melody (a little more complicated) over a syncopated accompaniment. This is a bossa nova beat, and you can study it in any Latin-based music book, or by looking at the music and analyzing it. But I warn you, it is complicated unless you feel it first.

We can make our simple I, IV, V accompaniment more interesting, however, by just changing the rhythm a tiny bit. Play the broken chords in a pattern of half note followed by two quarter notes: 1-2, 3,4; 1-2, 3,4. When you play the G major chord, play two quarter notes and hold the third note for six beats. Lonnng, short, short; Lonnng, short, short; short, short, Loooonnng. This whole pattern fills the time of four measures of 4/4 time.

- This is a slightly syncopated version of the accompaniment figure.

SIMPLE TUNES TO ACCOMPANY
Fewer words and more music!

I can use folk tunes and eighteenth- and nineteenth-century pieces in this book, but for more recent popular and classical pieces you must go to a music store, or to an online music store. There are usually three levels of arrangements: beginner, intermediate, and advanced. You will need to examine the music to see what you can handle—the beginner or intermediate arrangements.

If you purchase a popular tune because it looks simple enough to play, you may find, when you play it at home, that it sounds a bit "square" and uninteresting. There are two reasons for this: 1. You don't have a band to back you up; and 2. All the syncopations are deleted so it will be easy to read.

Practice the music until it feels easy and you are comfortable with it. Then play along with a recording, if you have it. This

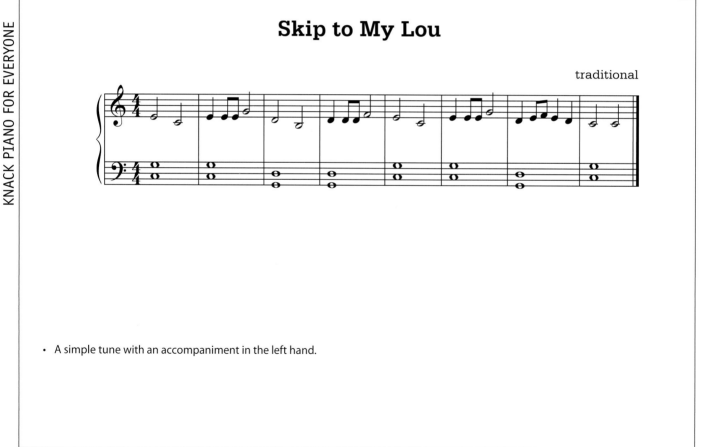

Skip to My Lou

traditional

- A simple tune with an accompaniment in the left hand.

will help you add some rhythmic pizzazz, and will make you feel as if you are part of the band! If you don't have a recording, play it as you hear it in your head. The main clue here is: You must feel comfortable playing it; it has to be easy.

Use your ear to try and pick out simple tunes, like "When the Saints," "This Land Is Your Land," and "Yellow Submarine." If you have a favorite tune on your iPod, play along with it to find one or two notes that fit the tune. Keep trying!

When you have a tune you can play (or whistle), make up a simple two- or three-chord accompaniment in the left hand.

You can use blocked chords or 5ths and 6ths. You can break up the chords and fit the accompaniment to the melody.

Skip to My Lou

traditional

- The same tune transposed to D major.

CHORDS FOR OTHER TUNES
A chord progression to accompany hundreds of tunes

Whether it is "Stormy Weather," "Earth Angel," "Mean to Me," or "Heart and Soul," these chords go with (at least) the beginning of many songs. If you listen to a lot of 1950s rock and roll, you will find more songs that fit. So get used to moving from one chord to another, repeating, without losing a beat. You can hold them for a couple of beats each.

The chords are: I, VI, IV (or II), V. In the key of C, that translates as C major, A minor, F major (or D minor), G major.

Practice playing each chord in both hands. The hands don't have to play at the same time. Set up a slow rhythmic beat and play the chords, left, right, left right. Experiment playing the IV or F major chord in the pattern; then play the D minor or II chord in the pattern. Which do you like the best? After you decide, practice the chord progression slowly; the first

C Major Chord, Both Hands

- Both hands are in a good playing position, with tall pinky, slanted thumb, strong palm (a good "dome").

- Take this opportunity to name the notes in the chord, up and down.

- Play the chord broken, one hand at a time, from the bottom up, then from the top down. Follow this with a blocked chord.

A Minor Chord, Both Hands

- As before, name the notes of the chord (or sing!) up and down.

- Each hand needs to practice the chord broken, from the bottom up, from the top down. Follow this with the blocked chord.

- Practice the move from the C chord to the A minor chord, back and forth slowly so you can get your hands in position on time.

time, hang on to each chord two long beats (or four short beats). When this feels comfortable and easy, halve the time, one long beat per chord (or two short beats). Now play it one short beat per chord. Add a little rhythm by repeating each chord with a long-short rhythm. Any two-syllable word will help you along—ma-jor, ma-jor, mi-nor, mi-nor. "Humpty Dumpty" is a good reminder.

The next step is to play the bass note (or name of the chord) in the left hand, the chord in the right hand. Keep your humpty-dumpty rhythm!

You can use the 2nd finger of the left hand for all its notes, or you can figure out a logical fingering in which your left hand will not have to move. Then you can concentrate on the right hand jumping to each chord.

F Major Chord, Both Hands

- Practice this chord (or the D minor chord) like you did the others.

- Now practice the move from C down to A, down to F (or up to D).

G Major Chord, Both Hands

- Practice this chord like the others.

- Practice one hand playing all four chords; then repeat the progression without stopping.

- Give the other hand a chance to practice those chords; repeat without stopping.

A TWO-HAND ACCOMPANIMENT
Make it more interesting by playing with two hands

Practice playing the chord progression in both hands, either separately or together. Then have the left hand play just the bass notes—C, A, F, G, with fingers 1-3-5-4 (or C, A, D, G with fingers 2-4-1-5). This fingering can be adjusted to 1-2-4-3, if it is easier for you. Be sure to try both ways. Also, you can play the bass notes with one finger, preferably finger 2. But when

you begin hands together, I think you might be glad to have the left hand stay in one place.

Now combine the left hand bass notes with the chords in the right hand. Don't play them simultaneously; play bass, chord, bass, chord, left, right, left right. Keep a steady, slow beat. Invite a friend or family member to play along with you,

- This tune is in my head, swimming around as I hear these chords. I don't know what it is or where I heard it; perhaps I learned it at Girl Scout camp!

- The tune fits the chords you have just learned; hold each bass note and each right hand chord one long beat, to coordinate tune and accompaniment.

on either the upper part of the piano, or on a melody instrument like flute, saxophone, trumpet, or violin. This could get to be serious fun! You are playing duets!

When you are playing with another person, your ability to "keep playing no matter what" will come in very handy. This is the time to forgive yourself the mistakes and keep the rhythm. No one cares if you make mistakes as long as you keep your part up. In fact, no one *knows* you make mistakes if you don't stop and just keep going. If no one is playing with you, record yourself playing the melody below; then play it back and accompany yourself. It's great practice!

If you don't have the ability to record yourself on your keyboard, or you don't have one of those cute little modern recording devices, what do you do? The cheapest answer is to sing the melody and accompany yourself.

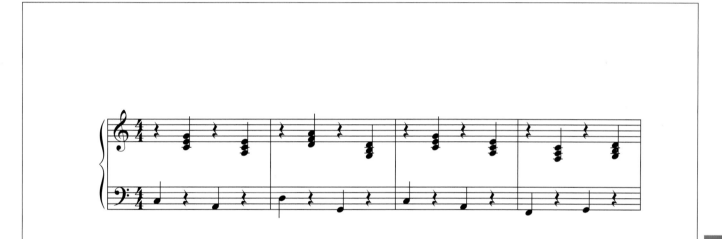

- These are the chords to accompany the melody I wrote out. I encourage you to find other tunes to fit the chords; I have mentioned a few of them already.

- Use the rhythm that you already set up—bass, chord, bass, chord.

- Of course, you can make up tunes, too!

TRANSPOSE!

Just when you thought you had conquered the mountain, I am asking you to climb another one

Doesn't the song say, "Climb ev'ry mountain"? So get ready to play your chord accompaniment in the key of G (the second mountain). First play the scale of G major up and down, in each hand. Then play the scale in double 3rds. Each hand gets a chance! Next play the primary chords in the key of G major: I = G, IV=C, V=D. Play them in each hand, until you feel comfortable moving to each chord. Now name the bass notes and practice those in the left hand. Then, put it together! You can combine the left hand bass and the right hand chord to fit any time signature, or any beat. Left-right-left-right is 2/4 time (the equivalent of bass-strum-bass-strum in guitar accompaniment). Left-right-right becomes 3/4 time.

G Major Chord, LH Bass Note

- The model is playing the G major chord in the right hand, the bass note in the left hand.

- In this picture, the lower part of the piano is being used (in case someone can play the melody in the treble), and the left hand thumb is on low G.

- The right hand chord is just below and just above middle C.

E Minor Chord, LH Bass Note

- Now the pianist has moved down to the E minor chord.

- The right hand has to move, so the left hand is using a fingering in which he will not have to move.

- Practice the progression from G major to E minor, one hand at a time, hands together, until if feel easy.

158

Practice hands alone as you work out this new key. Left hand plays the keys G-E-C(or A)-D. The right hand plays the chords G major, E minor, C major (or A minor), and D major. Don't forget the F♯ in the D chord!

When this becomes comfortable and sounds even (no stopping!), add a little rhythmic interest. Use the rocking rhythm you used before, or play bass note in the left hand, broken chord in the right hand, from the bottom up.

C Major Chord, LH Bass Note

- The piano player's left hand, finger 5, is on low C. His right hand plays the C chord an octave below middle C.

- Practice moving among the three chords in the right hand. Practice left hand playing fingers 1-3-5.

D Major Chord, LH Bass Note

- Now comes the really different part: the D major chord has F♯, but the left hand just plays D.

- Now that you have the whole sequence, practice it over and over; don't stop, but keep repeating.

PUT IT TOGETHER

SAME TUNE IN F MAJOR
Next mountain . . .

The key of F major has a different aspect with the B-flat as one of the bass notes. You need to practice the left hand playing F, D, B-flat, C, with fingers 1, 2, 4, and 3. Play it slowly about seven times to really get the feel of the pattern.

Try using the G minor chord instead of the B-flat major chord. The left hand will have it easier, playing F-D-G-C, with fingers 2-4-1-5.

The right hand will be affected also. When you move from the D minor to the B♭ major chord, you go forward toward the fallboard, to get the thumb on B♭. You can move to the G minor chord with less effort. Practice both ways several times to learn which set of chords feels the best. Try them in conjunction with the other chords; where you are coming from and where you are going to make a difference in your fingering.

F Major Chord, LH Bass Note

- Play the scale of F major with both hands. In the right hand the 4th finger will play B♭.

- Play the F major chord, one note at a time, saying or singing the names of the notes. Let both hands play the chord.

- Now play the chord blocked, both hands; then blocked in the right hand, bass note F in the left hand.

D Minor Chord, LH Bass Note

- Practice the chord like the F major chord. End with the chord in the right hand, the bass note, D, in the left hand, finger 2.

- Play back and forth between the F major and D minor chords in right hand, the F and D notes in the left hand.

These practice tips are good for learning any piece of music in which there are shifts for either hand or for both hands.

If you are getting tired of the same old exercise, same old sound, try a different one. Play the A minor (harmonic or melodic—your choice) scale, then play a triad on every note of the minor scale. This is certainly different! There are interesting possibilities if you change the form of the minor scale—from natural, to harmonic, to melodic. When you get used to this sound and this feel in A minor, try D minor (the relative minor of F major).

Choose the I, IV, and V chords: D minor, G minor, A major (or minor). Again, these are interesting sounds. You can play with these chords in this minor key by doing other five-finger exercises, and accompanying the chords with their bass notes.

B-Flat Major Chord, LH Bass Note

- Practice the B♭ major chord as you did F major and D minor. End with the chord in the right hand, bass note B♭ played in the left hand with finger 4.

- In left hand, repeat the note sequence, F, D, B♭, several times.

- Right hand practice moving from F major chord, to D minor chord, to B♭ chord several times.

C Major Chord, LH Bass Note

- The C major chord should be well practiced! Make sure it is easy to play the chord in the right hand, the bass note in the left hand with finger 3.

- Now practice the whole progression of chords—F major down to D minor, down to B♭ major, up to C major.

- Because of the black key in the left hand, play the bass notes F, D, B♭, C, with fingers 1, 2, 4, 3.

SAME TUNE IN D MAJOR

This is the last mountain for this tune (but you can try it in other keys)

After making you transpose the chords into different keys without any music, I have written out the chords in D major, using both chord progressions: I, vi, ii, V and I, vi, IV, V. You can practice them as you did the other keys. Be sure to plan which fingering you will use in the left hand.

I also wrote another melody that can go with these chords. Analyze it, plan the fingering, and away you go!

This is a good time to review key signatures. In the key of D major, two sharps are needed to make the scale sound like a major one—F♯ and C♯. These two sharps go into the key

- The hands do not play together in this accompaniment.

- Practice each hand separately, especially the right hand.

- I wrote a key signature instead of placing a sharp sign in front of each F and C when it appears.

signature at the beginning of each line of music. You won't need to put a sharp sign in front of every F and C.

The order of the sharps (or flats) in the key signature follows the order of sharp (or flat) additions around the circle of 5ths, clockwise for the sharps, counter-clockwise for the flats. The sharps' placement on the staff is orderly: F#, down a 4th C#, up a 5th G#, down a 4th D#, up a 5th A#, down a 4th E#, up a 5th B#. Because of the confusion in the ledger lines, A# and B# are written an octave lower.

The flats' placement on the staff is B♭, up a 4th, E♭, down a 5th, A♭, up a 4th, D♭, down a 5th, G♭, up a 4th, C♭, down a 5th, F♭.

Music in the traditional genres have these key signatures, always in the same order. If there are two sharps, the key signature has F# and C#. If there are three sharps, they are F#, C#, and G#, etc.

- There is a key signature instead of placing a sharp sign in front of each F and C as it appears.

- To remind you that certain notes are sharp, circle them with a pencil.

RHYTHMS FOR ACCOMPANIMENTS

You are beginning to sound like you know what you are doing!

As you get more comfortable with these chords, in these keys, make your playing a little jazzier, or swingier (is that a word?). Use the following rhythm: quarter, eighth, quarter, eighth (the quarter note is held twice as long as the eighth note) in each hand, first the left hand bass note, then the right hand chord ("Humpty Dumpty").

Next, using the same rhythm pattern, play broken chords in the right hand, after the bass plays on beat one.

In your one-man band, you are the rhythm section and the bass section!

For more ideas on accompanying, or "comping" as jazz musicians say, listen. In jazz listen to how many different ways

- The basic accompaniment in the key of C major.

- Notice the rests in each hand, which indicate that the hands do not play simultaneously.

chords are played. Listen to rock music, or to some traditional folk music. Hear what the guitarist, or mandolin player, or accordion player, or pianist is doing with the chords you just learned. Don't forget folk dance music. The folk dancers need the steady accompaniment of rhythmic music; there are plenty of recordings of traditional dance music for all kinds of folk dancing, from American square dancing to Cajun, to Balkan, to Irish reels and jigs, to English country, to Northeast contra dancing.

Another kind of music to listen to is choral music. When they are not singing a cappella (unaccompanied) they are usually being accompanied by a pianist or organist. What the accompanist plays to keep the singing moving and provide a good bass should be of interest to you.

- A suggested way to play the accompaniment.

- The hands are not playing together.

- The right hand is playing broken chords.

165

CONNECT I & V (BOTH HANDS)
Now that you are comfortable with jumping from chord to chord . . .

Recall playing the interval of a 6th and making sure the "gap" was between thumb and finger 2? You are going to fill in that 6th with another note to complete a triad that is inverted. You can play that inverted triad—let's say it is G major—right after you have played the C major chord, root position, with the left hand. Notice the moves as you play from the C to G chords. Left hand fingers 5 and 3 move down, away from the thumb, which

stays on its note. You are finding the note that is common between those two chords, and leaving it in the same "voice."

Play back and forth between C and G major, I and V, keeping the thumb on the G key. Close your eyes; you can now play from I to V with your eyes closed. Play the C major chord with the right hand. Move the thumb down to B, but leave the other fingers where they are. Play the G chord with fingers 1-2-5, on

Both Hands C Major Blocked Chord

- Relaxed hand position with curved fingers, elevated palm.

- You can refer to this photo anytime you need a picture of a good hand position.

- Left hand fingering: 5-3-1. Right hand fingering: 1-3-5.

Both Hands G Major Chord, 1st Inversion

- The key that is common between the chords stays in the same "voice."

- The other notes/keys move down to the nearest G major chord tone—finger 5 to B, finger 3 to D.

- The outside interval is a 6th. From the lowest key to the middle key is a 3rd. From the middle key to the highest key is a 4th.

- Left hand fingering: 5-3-1. Right hand fingering: 1-2-5.

the keys B-D-G. The gap, or 3rd, is still between fingers 1 and 2. This is a different feel, so practice the "smooth" move several times, slowly. Be sure to play this chord connection blocked and broken, slowly. Now try the chord connection in both hands at the same time. The right hand 3rd finger wants to play when the left hand finger 3 plays its part of the G chord. Go slowly. If this gets easier try it in a different key.

ZOOM

The term, "voices," indicates that all music is still closely connected to vocal music, and that we look at music horizontally as well as vertically. In a triad, the notes are called low or bass voice, middle voice, and high or treble voice. In hymn-style writing, whether it is for choir or four instruments, there are four voices: bass, tenor, alto, and soprano.

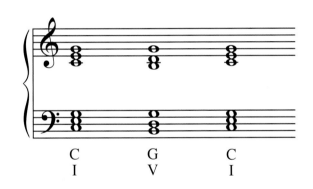

- Transpose the chords to F major. The connection involves no back keys.

SMOOTH CONNECTIONS

CONNECTING I & IV (BOTH HANDS)
Keep those chords under your hands

You don't have to jump around to find chords. As you get more familiar with the chords, the names of their notes, their different positions, you will get better and better at playing these smoothly connected progressions.

If you enjoy early rock and roll music, you can imitate some of the accompaniment figures the rock 'n rollers used. After you have practiced moving smoothly from I to IV, play each chord two times and continue playing them back and forth, rather fast with a staccato touch.

The smooth connection between I and IV involves the common note, C, that is in both chords. Leave it in the lowest place—in the left hand it will be finger 5—as you move only the thumb up to F. Then play fingers 5-2-1 in the left hand. The gap of a 3rd is still between fingers 1 and 2.

Both Hands, C Major Chord

- This is the same comfortable position as before.

- Practice the C major arpeggio. Start on the lowest note in the left hand, and play single notes all the way to the top voice of the right hand.

- Start at the top and play down the arpeggio.

- Use the damper pedal to make this sound rich and full.

Both Hands, F Major Chord, 2nd Inversion

- The lines show the movement of each voice.

- The common tone between the C chord and F chord is C, so it remains as the lowest voice.

- The other two voices move up to the nearest F major chord tones.

- Left hand fingering: 5-2-1. Right hand fingering: 1-3-5.

When the right hand moves to the IV chord, the thumb stays in place on C, fingers 3 and 5 move up to F and A. Play the chord with fingers 1-3-5.

Before trying this hands together, make sure each hand is adept at moving and playing from I to IV and back. When the hands play at the same time, go slower so the mind can compute what is happening.

Before moving this exercise to another key, try playing I-IV-I-V-I, smoothly connected in one hand, in the key of C. Set a slow rhythmic pulse and play steadily, two beats per chord if you prefer. When you feel like you have conquered the exercise in one hand, practice the same in the other hand.

Try playing G7 (V7) in this progression (instead of G major). Left hand plays (from the bottom) B-F-G. Do you like the sound better, or do you prefer the sound of plain V in the progression?

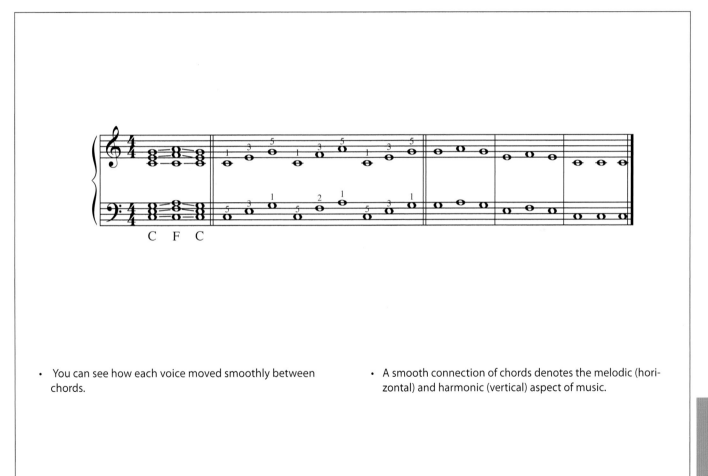

- You can see how each voice moved smoothly between chords.

- A smooth connection of chords denotes the melodic (horizontal) and harmonic (vertical) aspect of music.

CONNECT I, IV & V
Experiment with the progression in other keys

Remember to play the E major scale before you practice the chords in the key of E major.

Name the tones in the E major chord, then the A major. Which note is in both chords? Leave that note in place (in this case, the lowest voice), and move from the E major chord to the nearest A major chord tones, A and C♯.

Practice playing from the E major chord to the B major chord, back and forth, at least seven times. When it feels comfortable, play the chords E, A, E, B, E. Play those slowly until they sound rhythmically even and feel easy.

Now play the E, A, B, E major chords. Between A and B there are no common tones, so move to the B major chord that you used before. You need to know exactly where B major lies so you can go directly to it.

E Major Chords in Both Hands

- The G♯ in this chord makes it easy to form a relaxed hand shape.

- Name the notes as you play an arpeggio up and down.

- Start an octave lower and play an arpeggio that goes all the way up the keyboard; play hand over hand.

B Major Chords, 1st Inversion, Both Hands

- To connect smoothly, the V chord is played in the first inversion.

- The hands go forward to get the 5th finger and the thumb on black keys.

- Left hand fingering: 5-3-1 or 5-4-1.

After getting used to the chord connections, try the connections in a minor key. Since you have been playing in E major, play in the key of E minor. Play the scale first (it is relative to G major), then pick out the I, IV, and V chords. Notice that the IV and the V chords can be major or minor, according to the form of minor scale you use. Experiment with the V chord being minor, then major; experiment with IV chord being minor, and major. Try these minor key chords in the usual progression: E, A, E, B, E. Play the B chord minor, then major. Play the A chord minor, then major.

Play these chords of E minor with a bass accompaniment. Play the name of the chord in the left hand: E, A, E, B, E. When the left hand alone feels easy, play the bass in the left hand with the chords in the right hand. Experiment with the B chord being major and minor, the A chord being major and minor. Which sound do you like best?

E Major Chords, Root Position, Both Hands

- Take this opportunity to review the E major five-finger pattern.

- Play up the pattern and down, hands together.

- Now play the pattern in contrary motion.

- Play the E major and B major chords, smoothly connected, hands separately five times, hands together five times.

A Major Chords, 2nd Inversion, Both Hands

- Left hand 1 and right hand 5 move to C♯.

- This will probably make left hand finger 2 and right hand finger 3 move a little toward the fallboard as they play the note A.

- Black key fingers should play on the front edge of the keys.

- Stay relaxed; keep wrists and arms straight.

SMOOTH CONNECTIONS

HOW IT LOOKS ON PAPER
You can follow each voice in a linear fashion

You may want to play the E, B, and A major chords with different fingering. Be sure to use the thumb on every chord, and move forward on the keys to get the thumb on a black key. You want to move as little as possible when you change chords, so use a fingering that doesn't move the fingers too much.

When you get used to the move, play a little 1950s rock and roll with I and IV, two times for each chord. Try single bass notes in the left hand, E with the E major chord, A with the A major chord; or just use E in the bass for both chords. Jerry Lee, move over!

There is a song in *Grease* that celebrates the I, IV, and V

KNACK PIANO FOR EVERYONE

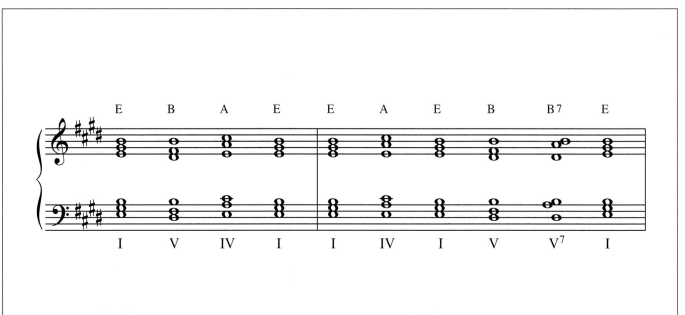

• Follow each voice as it moves, or repeats in the progression.

• When you play from the A major chord to the B major chord, there are no common tones. You simply move down (sometimes up—experiment!) to the nearest B major chord tones.

172

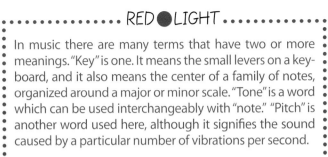

chords. If you have a recording, or if you can download one, it might be fun to try and play along with your chords.

As you look at the chords written out below, try singing the soprano line, throughout the progression. It sounds like B, C♯, B, B. Now follow the middle, or alto voice: G♯, A, F♯, G♯. The lower voice is E, E, D♯, E. No matter what key you play this progression in, the tune is the same.

Oh! Susanna

S. Foster

- Here is a familiar tune (!) with an accompaniment of smoothly connected chords.

START IN DIFFERENT POSITIONS
This is for the thinking person who wants to master this chord progression

Practice one hand at a time, please. You have to wrap your mind around the knowledge of the key, and your fingers around the chords.

You may play these chords in a different order: I, IV, I, V, I. Or you may play I, IV, V, I. Write out these progressions on music paper so you can see the smooth connections.

Notice that when you play from the IV to V chords, there are no common notes; so the whole hand moves slightly to the nearest V chord.

Once you find it easy to play this progression, play it in other keys, particularly G, F, and D major. When those keys feel comfortable, change your left hand to just single bass

C Major Chord, 1st Inversion, Both Hands

- Practice this chord hands together in order to coordinate the fingering: 5-3-1 in left hand, 1-2-5 in right hand.

- Practice single notes hands together in contrary motion, then parallel motion.

- Move from root position to 1st inversion, hands separately, hands together.

G Major Chord, 2nd Inversion

- Name the notes in this chord, up and down.

- Because finger 2 of the right hand is already on G, the common tone, you may play the G chord with fingering 1-2-4.

- Play hands together, contrary motion, parallel motion.

- Move between the C major chord and the G major chord, in these inversions.

174

notes. You'll be playing chords in the right hand, bass notes in the left. The notes are the names of the chords; so in the key of C major, the left hand will play C, F, C, G, C; or C, F, G, C. You can play these with one finger, or a fingering that allows you to stay in the same hand position: finger 5 on C, finger 1 on G.

When you play the progression, try singing each voice in turn: soprano, middle, lower. Now you may be reminded of a song or two! Try finding the chords that go with the tune. Or, you can make up a tune that fits with the chords. Think of

a rhythmic drum beat and try playing your left hand and the right hand chords in that beat (not necessarily together—think of the drummer's technique).

There are many ways you can use these chords, aside from the few I have suggested. Soon you will be able to pick out chord outlines and skips in the music that you read.

C Major Chord, 1st Inversion, Both Hands

- Play back and forth between this chord and the G major chord 2nd inversion.

- Notice the location of the common tone, G; it is in the middle voice.

- Because finger 2 of the right hand is already on G, you may leave it there and play finger 4 on B when you move from the C chord.

F Major Chord, Root Position, Hands Together

- Since this is positioned just behind the C chord in 1st inversion, the left hand may use fingering 4-2-1. Practice both fingerings (5-3-1) in this chord progression to decide which you would rather use.

- Practice the chord progression with the chords in different order.

MUSIC
More tunes to accompany with smoothly connected chords

Why do I choose these tunes? I have several criteria: the tune must be simple but interesting; it should be a folk tune or a tune I make up; and it should be easy to transpose to other keys.

Once you start playing some of the pieces in this book, you will feel confident about choosing a book of songs you would

like to play. As I have said, don't choose a book in which the names of the notes are written on the noteheads.

When you begin to learn a piece, be sure to study, analyze, and plan the fingering of the melody. Make sure you can play the melody easily before putting a left hand part with it. If the left hand part seems too difficult at first, choose your

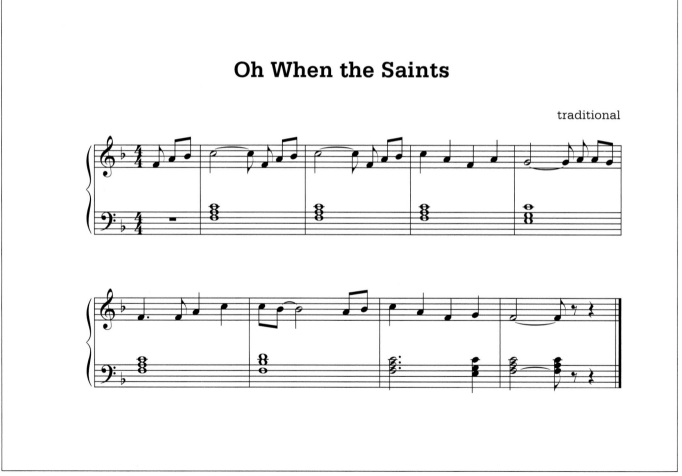

Oh When the Saints

traditional

own notes to play: a blocked 5th is a good beginning. Which blocked 5th? You need to know the key of your piece!

Once you have established the key, play the home key in the left hand to see if it sounds okay with the melody. When the melody seems to drift away from the home key, experiment with other notes in the left hand. Which ones sound okay? Can you get there easily from the original note?

All of this experimentation requires that you know and play the melody comfortably.

I am using a tune that I used before. The first time I accompanied with single notes. This time I am putting in the whole chord. Go back to tunes you have played before in this book; try out chords in the left hand. When you have decided which ones you can use, practice connecting the chords smoothly, until it feels easy. Then, try your accompaniment with the melody.

This Old Man

traditional

SMOOTH CONNECTIONS

ACCOMPANY WITH 5THS & 6THS

Accompany each note of the major five-finger pattern with either a 5th or a 6th

Your brain may be smoking from all that focus on keys and chords. Pull back a little and play a familiar five-finger pattern in the RH. Accompany each note with an interval of a 5th or a 6th. Play slowly and listen. Which combination sounds best? Can you reason why?

The secret is knowing which notes are triad tones. Once you know the triad tones, and the non-triad tones, you can accompany the triad tones with a 5th, the non-triad tones with a 6th.

Once you have perfected the accompaniment of the major five-finger pattern in C major, try it in G major. When you changed from 5th to 6th in the key of C, the left hand 5th

RH on C, LH on Blocked 5th

- When you accompany each note of the five-finger pattern, the left hand will play an interval of a 5th with triad tones.

- Name the triad notes in C major. Play each one with a P5th in the left hand.

- Now reverse—left hand play the triad notes, right hand play the P5th.

RH on D, LH on Blocked 6th

- Your left hand wants to move to a 6th when you play D in the right hand.

- Try both 6ths; the thumb moving away from the

hand, the fingers moving away from the thumb.

- Which one sounds the best? Do you know why?

KNACK PIANO FOR EVERYONE

178

finger moved down a half step (and the other fingers went along for the ride, making the gap between fingers 1 and 2). In G major, when your left hand switches from 5th to 6th, the fifth finger must move to F♯. Changing from 5th to 6th by moving the left hand thumb involves white keys only. In the key of F major you have only the white keys when you change to the 6th either way.

The key of D major is similar to G major, because, to move from a 5th to a 6th, the fifth finger (or thumb, in right hand) must go to a black key (C♯).

These 5ths and 6ths are the outside notes of triads and triad inversions. Think of the whole triad at least one time during this practice. Which middle key will it be? Can you think through it, or experiment with the sound by adding the one key in the middle?

Become immersed in these patterns accompanied by 5ths and 6ths. The easier they are, the easier the next step will be.

RH on E, LH on Blocked 5th

- Now the melody note is E. You can shift your left hand back to the 5th.

- Practice playing each note of the triad with the P5th in the left hand. Go up and down, play two notes at the same time.

RH on F, LH on Blocked 6th

- The right hand plays 4th finger on F.

- The left hand moves to a 6th. Try it both ways—

thumb away from fingers, fingers away from thumb

- Which 6th sounds the best? Why?

LEARN TO ACCOMPANY
Now use your ear and your knowledge to accompany a simple five-finger tune

Study and play the melody; decide where you want to accompany with a 5th or a 6th. Mark it under the melody notes. Play it hands together and listen. Do you like the sound?

There are many books in which there are simple melodies to play and to accompany. Look through music at your local music store, or do a search on the Internet. Beyond this, keep playing five-finger patterns and mixing up the notes. Instead of playing fingers 1-2-3-4-5 in the right hand, play fingers 1-3-2-4-3-5. Another mix can be 2-1-3-2-4-3-5. You can jot down these finger patterns in order to remember them and keep

- Here is a melody for which there is no accompaniment. On beat one of each measure decide if you want to play a 5th or a 6th.

- Mark in pencil on the 1st beat of each measure which interval you will use—5th or 6th.

- Is there a measure in which you will need to change the left hand halfway through the measure?

them right in front of you. You can reverse the patterns (5-3-4-2-3-1, for instance), or make new ones. Any one of these combinations might remind you of a familiar song.

Remember that for accompaniment you can use the perfect 5th all the way through the piece. The only decision you have to make is when to play it. Next, you can play one note of the 5th, or the other; i.e. finger 5 or finger 1. Again, you only have to decide which note sounds better in which measure.

The next step is to play 5ths and 6ths. Perhaps the change

will come in the same place you changed from finger 5 to finger 1 in the last version.

Go back in the book and play melodies that you played before. They are much easier now! Use the advice for accompanying to add a left hand part. Try just the P5th all the way through; then 5 finger or finger 1; then a blocked 5th or 6th.

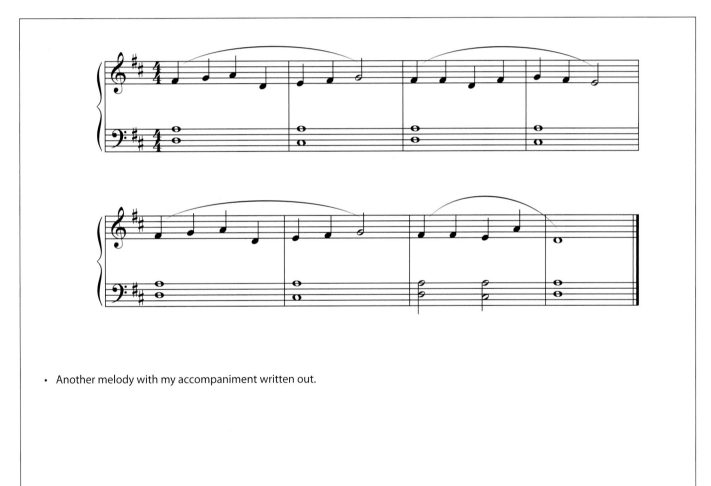

- Another melody with my accompaniment written out.

SWITCH HANDS
Another example of equal time for both hands

Your brain will really light up from this one! Can you play the melody in the left hand and accompany with 5ths and 6ths in the right hand? This is one way to get the hands-together routine going.

Another exercise is to play both hands up and down a five-finger pattern, right hand legato, left hand staccato. Try this at four beats to a note, then two beats, then one beat. When

this is getting easy, reverse: right hand staccato, left hand legato. Go through the same routine. Your brain is "smoking" now!

A trick I find helpful in my own practice is to play the left hand part of a particular piece with the right hand. You can move down the bench so that it is comfortable to play it straight in front of you, or you can play it an octave higher

LH G, RH P5th

- The left hand plays the melody note, G, with finger 5.

- The right hand accompanies with a P5th.

- Play up and down the triad in the left hand, while the right hand holds the P5th.

LH A, RH 6th

- The left hand plays the melody note, A.

- The right hand moves to a 6th to accompany.

- Try playing both 6ths—thumb away from fingers,

fingers away from thumb—to decide which sounds the best to you.

- Do you know the reason for your choice, besides the fact that you think it sounds better?

so you don't have to move. Now reverse: play the right hand part with the left hand, in a comfortable position.

Yet one more exercise: Play the right hand part fortissimo and the left hand part pianissimo. Then reverse that process.

If you ask pianists and piano teachers for their tips on practicing, these ideas and more will be suggested. Teachers have many different ways to get their pupils to reach the same goal: to play with ease and confidence and to achieve a rich sound up and down the keyboard.

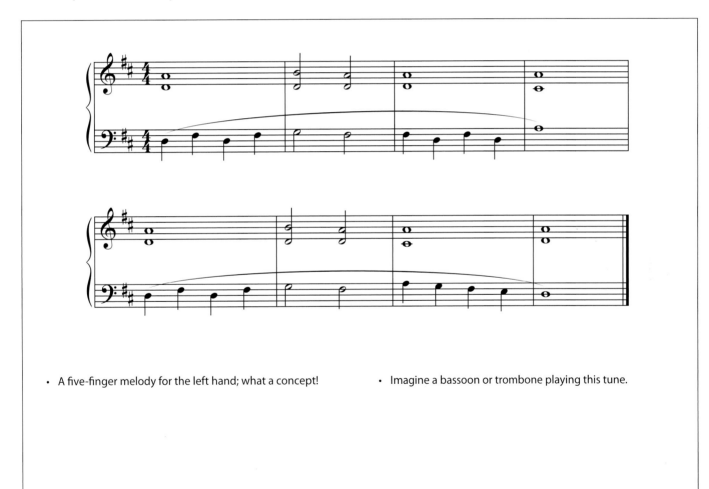

- A five-finger melody for the left hand; what a concept!
- Imagine a bassoon or trombone playing this tune.

ACCOMPANY THE MAJOR SCALE

Expand your melody to include each note of the major scale

You can play a 5th to a 6th by moving either the thumb away from the hand, or the fingers away from the thumb. After practicing this, play each note of the scale (C major is easiest at this point) in the right hand, and accompany each note with either the 5th, or one of the 6ths. Experiment with both 6ths; decide which one sounds the best to you, then try to reason why. By playing this 5th and 6th accompaniment, you are really playing I to V or I to IV, without the middle notes to complete the chords. Now you can play the whole chord with each melody note; you may change your mind about the choices of accompanying notes.

If you know the first phrase of "Joy to the World," you can

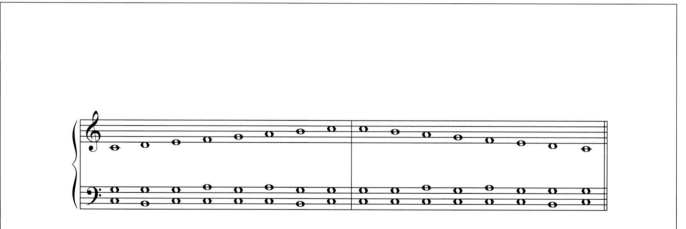

- The C major scale is in the right hand; your accompaniment of 5ths and 6ths is in the left hand.

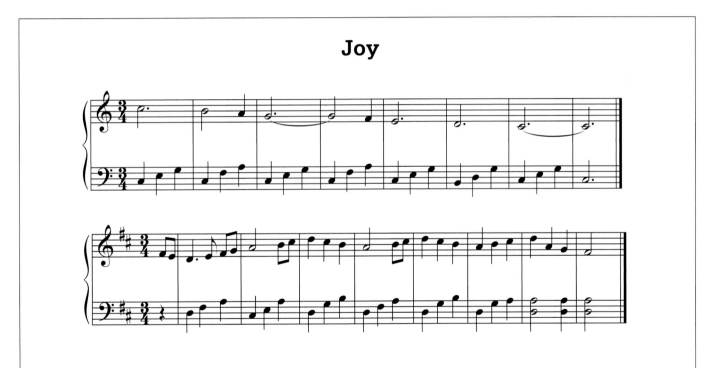
play it (it is a major scale descending) with the 5th-6th accompaniment. If this is easy, try the whole chord, played with each note.

If you know the first phrase of "The First Noel," you can play it (it is a major scale ascending, after the first two notes) with chord as accompaniment. Remember, you are filling in the middle note of the 5ths and 6ths. Since both these holiday songs have some fast notes, you don't have to accompany every note of the melody. "First Noel" is in 3/4 time, so play your accompanying chord, or 5th or 6th, on the word "first." The next accompanying figure plays with the syllable "-el." Do you feel the 1-2-3 of the rhythm?

"Joy to the World" is in 2/4. The left hand plays with the word "Joy," then "world." Or you can play on every beat of most measures. Try out different ways to accompany, including single notes in the bass (just the name of each chord).

Joy

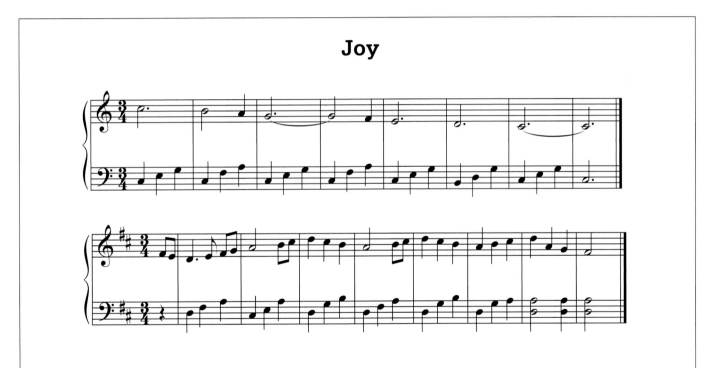

- Keep playing up the scale with the accompaniment in the left hand.

- When this starts to feel easy, you can do two things: go faster, or change keys.

185

CHALLENGE YOUR BRAIN!

Light up your brain; switch hands

Now it is time to put the scale in the left hand and accompany with the right hand. Make sure you can play the scale easily in the left hand. Then fit the 5th or the 6th to each note. On some notes both a 5th and a 6th fit nicely and sound good. You have to decide which one you prefer. Go slowly! Listen!

Other ways to challenge your brain: When you play the 5th in the left hand, play up the accompanying triad in the right hand. (RH plays C-E-G) On degree two of the scale, left hand will play a 6th, right hand will play D-F-G. Continue this way up the scale. When you have done this, put the scale back in the left hand, and therefore the triads, and the 5ths and 6ths

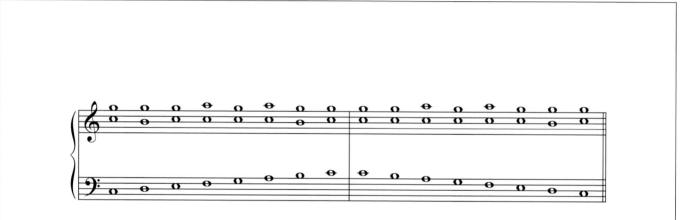

- I have written out the scale in the left hand, and indicated where the 5th or 6th should go.

in the right hand. Some of the combinations sound good, others do not sound as good. But it is fun to experiment.

Another way to have fun and challenge your brain is to play lots of broken chords, hand over hand, up and down the piano keyboard, with the damper pedal down. Play major, then minor chords. Be sure and let the pedal up between chords, so the sound does not get murky. Or you may like the murky sound. Go with it!

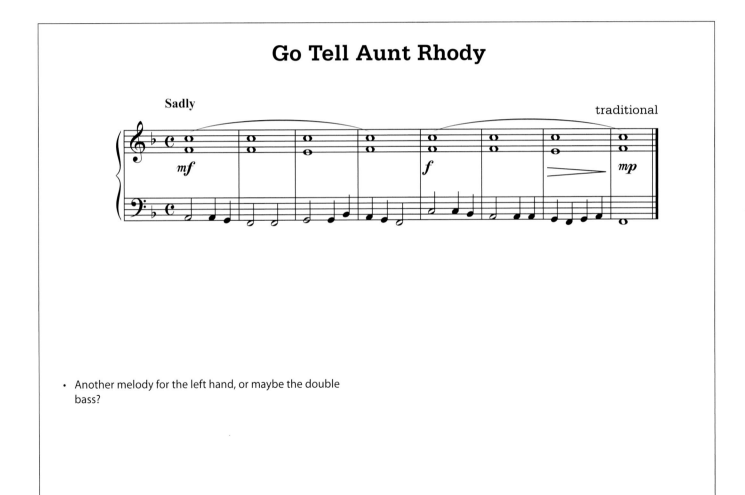

Go Tell Aunt Rhody

Sadly

traditional

- Another melody for the left hand, or maybe the double bass?

APPLY YOUR KNOWLEDGE
Now that you have rehearsed accompanying scale notes, transfer the knowledge to a real tune

Analyze the melody; practice it until it feels easy and comfortable. Plan the accompaniment by writing in a 5th or a 6th below notes where you think it will sound good. Practice the left hand alone until it feels easy. Now play the hands together. How does it sound? Make changes where needed.

If you have music paper, write out a tune that you can copy, or you can play on the piano. Plan an accompaniment the same way. Study the melody for triad tones (that is, the I chord), tones that are not in the triad, tones that are in other triads. Plan the spots for your accompaniment; mark it in the

music. Then play hands together. Fix the places that do not sound good. Play it again; keep a steady beat!

Can you change a tune from major to minor? Why not? It's a good exercise. Choose the parallel minor key; make sure you can play the scale of the minor key three ways: natural, harmonic, and melodic. Play one of the melodies below, or another tune you played before. The main adjustment is the third note of the scale; it has to be lowered a half step. Once that is done, the rest of the tune sounds minor no matter which form you use.

If you can play "Twinkle, Twinkle Little Star" easily, try it in minor. Since it uses only the first six notes of the scale, it is easy to change it to minor. Once that is mastered, accompany with a minor (I chord), a minor IV chord, and a major V chord. Or you can accompany with 5ths and 6ths.

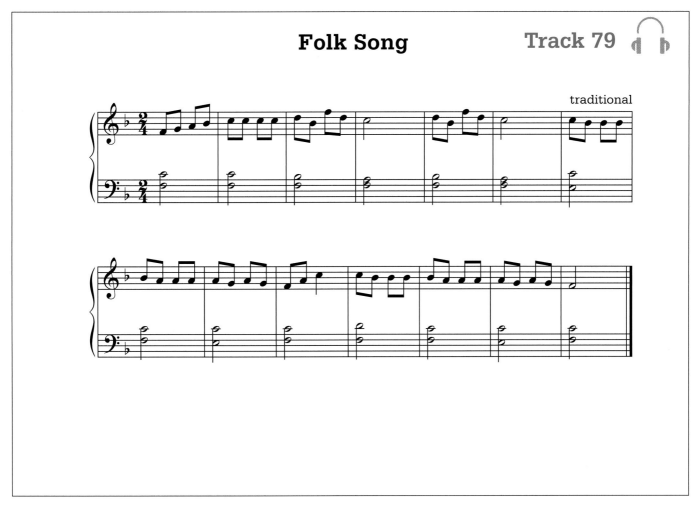

Folk Song   Track 79

traditional

189

SITTING TOGETHER

When you play duets with a partner, prepare for close company

Playing duets with a friend/partner is one of the most satisfying ways to make music. There are many duet books for your use, at all different levels. There is music in which one part is simpler than the other. There is music in which the parts are technically even.

Using one bench for two people feels a little crowded, but you will get used to it. Each of you should sit as close to the side (right or left) as is comfortable. The part of the music at the high end of the piano is the "*primo.*" The part of the music at the low end is the "*secondo.*"

You will find that the secondo right hand and the primo left hand are side by side, or even crossed in places. The two of you may need to decide which hand plays above and which under.

Two Pianists on One Bench

- It may take time to get really comfortable.

- Try to put a little space between you.

- You can communicate well because you are so close.

- Practice starting and ending your piece several times, until you both feel comfortable.

Two Pianists on Two Benches

- This option gives you a little more "wiggle" room.

- The primo left hand and secondo right hand have elbow room.

- If you have the opportunity, practice with both setups to decide which arrangement you are both comfortable with.

Sitting on two smaller benches or chairs can make playing a little easier and more comfortable. You can use two double benches and turn both 90 degrees. If you place the benches at an angle to the keyboard, with the side near the middle placed the farthest away from the keyboard, you may have more room for the inside arms and elbows.

Since there are two people playing, you should be sensitive to the loudness of the accompanying part. This may be in the primo left hand and/or the secondo right hand. Once you

have identified the accompaniment, try playing it at half the dynamic level. It will make the more important parts sound even more important!

March

Anton
Diabelli

MUSIC FOR DUETS
Primo and secondo; two ways to print the music

Some duet music is written on two pages; i.e., the primo part is on the right side, the secondo is on the left side. Duet music can also be printed with both parts on the same page; i.e., the primo part is printed above the secondo part so that you can see exactly how the parts fit together.

No matter how the music is printed, each person in the duo must learn his/her part thoroughly. When a pianist practices a duet part alone, he/she should sit on the side where he/she will sit with the partner; that is, if he is playing the secondo part, he should sit on the left side of the bench when practicing. Use a metronome to imitate playing with a partner.

If you have recording capabilities, record the other part so

Duet Music on One Page

- You can see exactly how both parts fit together.

- You need to put a bright mark at the beginning of each line of a given part; it is easy to get lost.

that you can practice hearing it when you practice alone.

Listen for the accompaniment parts—make sure they aren't drowning out the more important themes.

When you practice alone, the metronome may help take the place of a partner. Be sure to have it tick slowly enough for you to play easily, and try only one hand at a time.

When you are rehearsing with a partner, practice different combinations of hands separately: both right hands, both left hands, primo left hand secondo right hand, primo right hand secondo left hand. If a spot is hard to get together, both of you count out loud to make sure you are counting and feeling the passage the same way.

Practicing Your Duet Part Alone

- Be sure to sit on the side where you will eventually play with a partner.

- Use a metronome to give you a sense of keeping up with your partner.

- Mark in the music the places you will have to move fast or play with a high or low hand in order to get out of your partner's way.

More Tips for Practicing Your Duet Part

- Know your part 100 percent. Be able to play your part at several different tempos.

- Learn your partner's part, not perfectly, but enough to give you an extra-sensitive awareness of the other part.

- Make sure you can play one hand alone. Usually the secondo part needs the left hand to "stay in," and the primo part needs the right hand to "stay in," if for some reason you need a hand for something else (like turning a page).

193

PRACTICE TIPS
What else do you need to know?

You will want to practice your part, primo or secondo, until it feels easy. You will practice your part sitting on the appropriate side of the bench—on the right side for the primo, on the left side for the secondo.

When you first hear your part with the other pianist's part, it will actually feel differently, even though it is not. Be sure

to practice regularly with your partner in order to get used to hearing the whole piece. This is where recording capabilities are a help. If you can record your partner's part you can practice with it when alone.

All the practice aids you have learned and used so far will help you with your part. Watch out for clef signs; go through

Down in the Valley

Primo

Secondo

Track 82

traditional

• A not very complicated duet with both parts on the same page.

the music and circle the clef sign when it changes.

When you sit on the appropriate side to play your part, notice where middle C is. Your orientation to the keyboard has completely changed! When you have practiced your part thoroughly, and you are playing with your partner, you won't notice the change in orientation.

If you and your partner are not used to playing together, try playing a slow scale together, either one hand or both. You will have to communicate your tempo, when you start, when you end. It's an excellent way to get started.

Decide before your first rehearsal together at what tempo you need to practice the piece, and what the final tempo will eventually be. (This can change, but it is helpful to have a sense of where you are headed.)

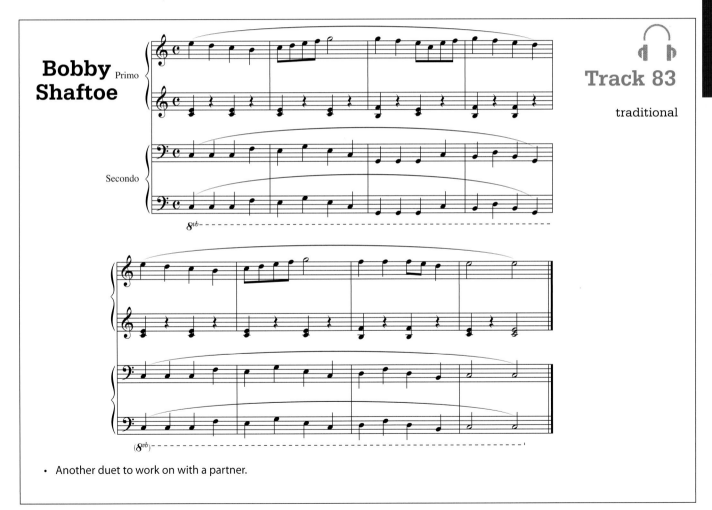

Bobby Shaftoe Primo

Secondo

Track 83

traditional

• Another duet to work on with a partner.

MORE TIPS FOR DUET PLAYING
I should be an expert, but . . .

When you are playing with a partner, make sure you keep in contact with the other person. (This goes for playing with one or more singers, or another instrumentalist.) You don't necessarily have to look at each other (you are too busy looking at your music!), but you can sense the other person. Practice starting and ending a piece together. You must have your hands ready on the keys, feel the pulse (can you sense your partner's rhythmic pulse?), and breathe together for that first note. You don't have to make a sound, but you both need a sense of the upbeat before the first note.

You may have trouble sounding that first note together. When you rehearse, both of you look at your hands to see how you "attack" the beginning note(s). It is always helpful to see the hands playing. Make sure you decide who the leader

Duet Pianists Ready to Begin

- The two partners are looking at each other; their hands are ready on the first keys.

- They can take a quiet breath as an upbeat to beginning the piece.

- The breath can be accompanied by a subtle lift of the wrist; this will help indicate the tempo.

- It is best not to count to start the duet. You should have a sense of the tempo from all your rehearsing!

Crossing Hands

- There are times when the secondo right hand has to cross over the primo left hand in order to play his/her notes, or vice versa.

- At rehearsal it must be decided which hand plays low (under the other hand) and which hand plays high.

- There are issues with elbows also. These things have to be worked out at rehearsals. Remember— how it sounds is the ultimate test.

will be. This person gives the upbeat breath, and lifts the wrist in anticipation of the first note. Also, the two of you have to decide who will signal for ritardando, and for the ending.

Page turning can be troublesome. Sometimes the choice of who turns the page is obvious, but there are times when both parts are so busy that neither of you can spare a moment for a page turn. You can do two things about it: 1. Copy the pages you will need, tape them to the appropriate sides, and turn at the next convenient place; 2. Both of you memorize

your parts at that place. You might find it convenient to turn before the difficult spot or after the difficult spot. The two of you must decide and take care of the problem.

Be sure to label who turns at the bottom of each page to be turned.

- Here is the music in which the partners' hands have to cross.

MUSIC FOR DUET PLAYING
Coordinate with your partner by learning both parts of the duet

The composing of piano duets parallels the history of the piano. By the time the piano became more popular than the harpsichord, in the 1770s, the publication of piano duets equaled that of piano solos. Famous composers of solo piano music also wrote duets. Wolfgang Mozart and his sister, Nannerl, played duets in concerts.

Duet playing was popularized during the golden age of piano manufacturing. By the mid-1800s the middle classes of European countries and America felt the need of a musical pastime, and playing the piano was among the more prominent means to this end. Many composers realized the market for duet music was growing.

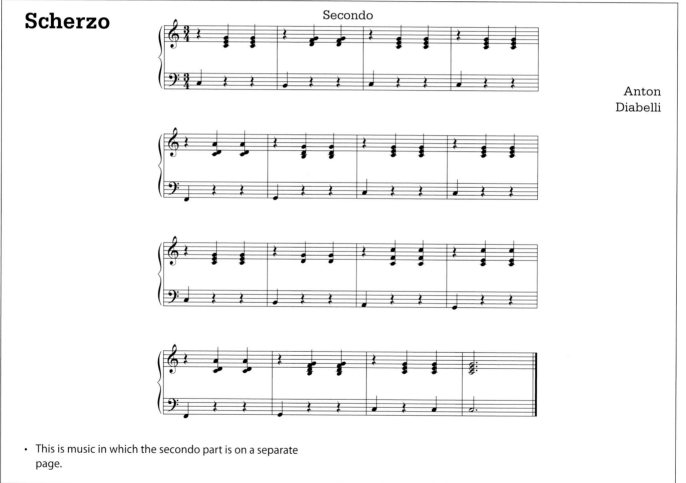

Scherzo

Secondo

Anton
Diabelli

- This is music in which the secondo part is on a separate page.

Since there was no radio, nor were there recordings, composers saw a quick way to get their orchestra compositions known. Therefore there are many orchestra pieces, and symphonies, in a piano-duet reduction. You can find all the Beethoven symphonies and all the Brahms symphonies in piano-duet arrangements.

When you practice the duet below, learn both parts, so that you and your partner can switch places. It is always helpful to know what the other person has to contend with. If you know the music of both parts completely, you will make an even better duet partner!

This is especially true if the primo and secondo parts are on separate pages. You will need to know what the other part sounds like since you can't really see it; and even if you play the part, it is difficult to see how the parts line up.

All these problems will get worked out in rehearsal. The most important thing is that you enjoy the music, your partner, working on something you like, and seeing results.

DUETS=FUN

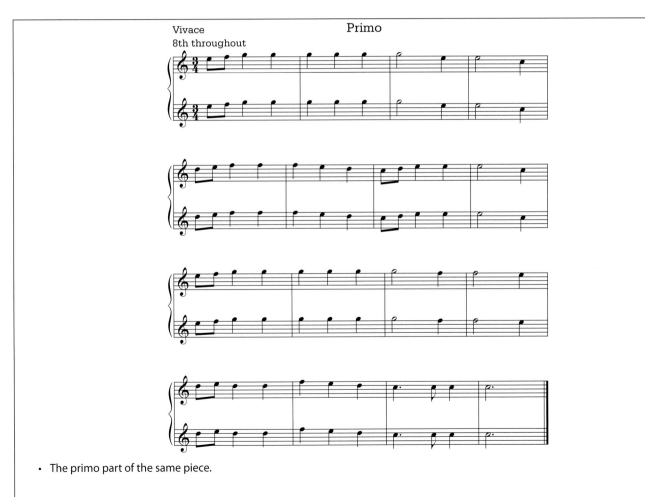

- The primo part of the same piece.

MORE MUSIC FOR DUET PLAYING
Use your digital piano or computer to record the other part

If you have recording capabilities, now is the time to use them. Learn both parts of the duet, and record one or both parts. Then play it back and play along on the duet part. Have your partner record the part he/she is playing, slowly. Use this recording to practice the duet alone.

You may be pleasantly surprised, or disappointed. If re-cording is easy for you, record some of your solos. Don't feel discouraged or overconfident; just use the recording as a way of improving your playing. The recording is not a judge!

Try playing along with any recording. If you know the key of the piece you can practice the primary notes, I, IV, and V, and even the primary chords, then try playing a note or a chord

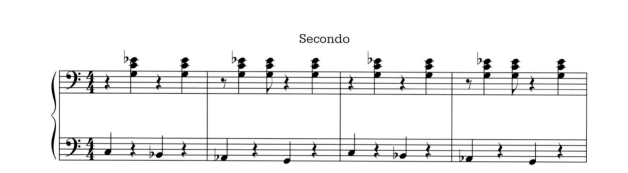

Secondo

- The music is separated by putting the primo part on the right page, the secondo on the left page.

- This may make it easier to read for the individual, but you cannot see the other pianist's part.

- Repeat these 4 measures until Primo is finished.

where you sense it should be. Many folk and rock musicians learn their art by playing along with a very good recording, or a very old recording (from the Library of Congress, for example).

For duet playing, try the folk duet, "Chopsticks." There are only two chords for the bottom part, G major and C major, and the top part can be learned from many people. The timing is three beats per measure. Playing this will get you accustomed to ensemble playing and to hearing the balance.

There are other duets that you can try, one in a major key, one in a minor key that is a little jazzy. The main theme of the primo part to this last one (I have no name for it) begins by ascending a minor five-finger pattern, from C up to G. The secondo has a C minor triad in the right hand, a descending bass line which is C, B-flat, A-flat, G. Play bass-chord, bass-chord in a steady 4/4 beat.

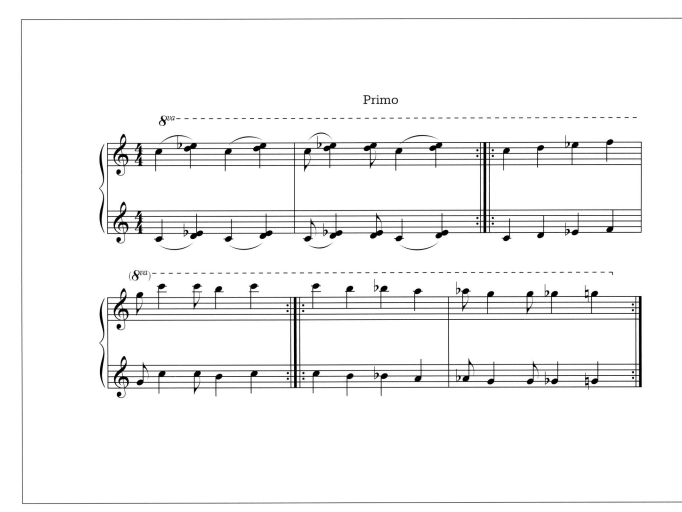

Primo

PRACTICE TIPS
Organize in your mind, or organize on paper. You need a plan

There are several books on organizing your practice time, if you feel the need for help in that area. I prefer to spend a certain amount of time warming up my fingers and hands. Then I go over difficult spots I know I must conquer. It may not happen in one day, but if I persevere I will get it right, at the right tempo.

I don't need to write down very much because I've been doing this almost all my life. When I practice to re-learn the pieces I give students, I do need to write down my own assignment. Because this is new for you, you may need some guidance, either from a planned assignment sheet or your own plan.

A Sample Practice Journal Page

WEEKLY LESSON PLAN

TODAY'S DATE:

SCALES AND WARMUPS	SPECIFIC GOALS
ETUDES AND EXERCISES	SPECIFIC GOALS
REPERTOIRE	SPECIFIC GOALS
OTHER	SPECIFIC GOALS

- Here is one page from a printed journal made especially for musicians.
- This gives a place for weekly assignments and goals.
- The goals include tempos; you have to set a tempo goal for each piece.

On Back of That Page . . .

- Across from the first page is a place for writing observations, smaller goals, etc., for each day.
- This page is probably where the work gets done. You are asked to listen, question, and comment on your practice session.

In planning for practice time, don't say that when you finish such-and-such, if there is time left you will practice. If this is a guideline for choosing a practice time, you will never practice! Write it in your daily schedule. It may vary as to length of time, but at least you will sit at the piano and practice something. If you are serious about learning to play, you have to commit serious time for practice.

Practicing is such a personal activity, and it can be lonely. You may need a friend who is also playing piano to play duets with. When you are feeling successful at your new hobby, try playing for someone close to you—family or friend. It gives a whole new perspective to practicing!

There are piano camps for adult piano students, from beginners on up to advanced. At one of these you will get private lessons and a chance to play in front of an audience.

There are also guides for practicing piano, in book form or leaflet form.

- These are the warm-up exercises I do when I practice.

- I do not always do them the same way, or at the same tempos.

- I never look at music when I am warming up. I need the exercises to be simple enough to allow me to concentrate on how my hands look and feel.

USE YOUR KNOWLEDGE

HOW DOES IT FEEL?

The way you sit at the piano or keyboard makes a difference in your playing

I often tell my students, no matter what age, to sit tall. Inevitably the music they are playing sounds better. When you are well balanced on the bench or chair, feet apart on the floor or right foot on the damper pedal, sitting tall, the weight you have behind your fingers helps you to produce a better tone on the piano.

Even when you are practicing the exercises, five-finger patterns, scales, or chords, you need to be aware of your position and how you are sitting. If you are sitting correctly you won't tire as easily. If you are relaxed you will have more stamina.

Check the height of your piano bench. The arms, when playing, need to be parallel to the floor. If they are not, you

- The pianist's forearms are parallel to the floor.
- His back is straight.

- The pianist is sitting on the front half of the bench.
- His feet are flat on the floor.

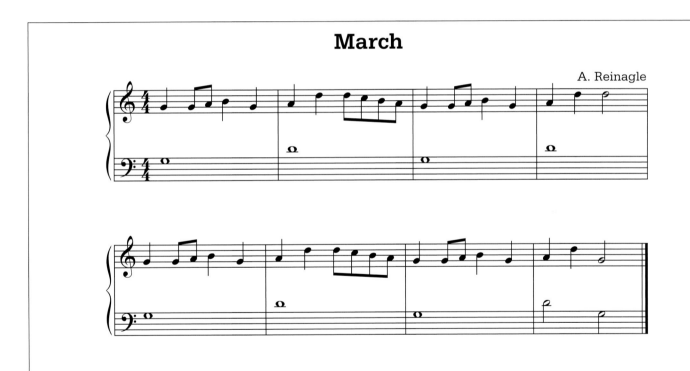

need to either change the bench or chair to a lower one, or stack a pillow or two on the bench to make you higher.

Now check your distance from the keyboard. You need room to move your arms freely, out, in, up, down. Don't sit far back on the bench; you should only use the front half. This makes for more comfortable pedaling and playing. Your hands and arms should feel free to float above the keyboard, and to easily move up and down the keyboard.

When your sitting posture is adjusted to perfection, look at a page of music. Can you see it clearly? Do you wear glasses to read books and newspapers? These are often not good for music reading, since the music stand is farther away. I use reading glasses for books, and different glasses for reading piano music and for working at the computer.

Bifocals can be a problem; you can see the music but the keyboard and your hands are a blur! These are things to discuss with your optometrist and other pianists.

March

A. Reinagle

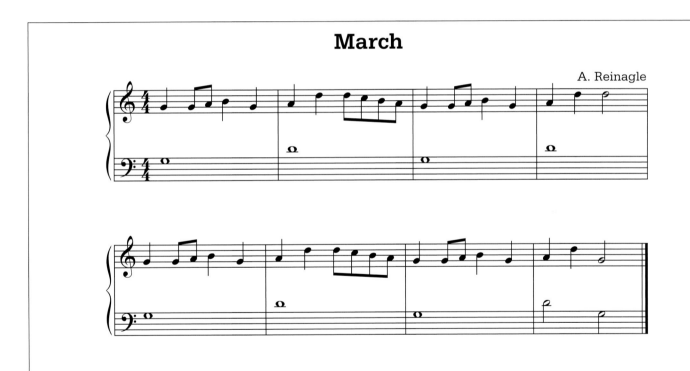

- A short, fairly simple classical piece by an early American composer.
- Analyze it.

205

SLOW & STEADY
How you practice makes you confident as a piano player

I have emphasized the importance of playing slowly throughout the book. It isn't just your fingers that you are training, but your brain, and you need to play a passage, an exercise, correctly seven times. You must play slowly so that the brain doesn't learn the mistakes too well!

For an excellent example of slow practice, read the section of Abram Chasins' book, *Speaking of Pianists*, about his visit to Rachmaninov.

I suppose the point is: slow enough for long enough. We all (me included!) have trouble in that area.

When you have practiced a piece for a couple of weeks, if you are feeling comfortable playing it, then sit down at the piano at a different time of the day and just play it. Don't think too hard. Let the muscle memory take over.

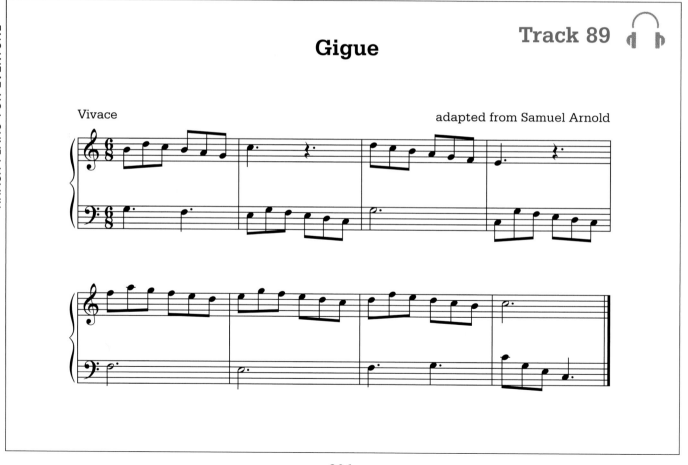

Track 89

Gigue

Vivace

adapted from Samuel Arnold

Mistakes will be made; we know this and accept this. We are only human. We are simply cutting down on the number of times we make mistakes, and on the number of mistakes.

There is a time in the practicing of a piece, in which you just play it, or in practicing a chord progression, you just play it, no thinking, no worrying, just play it. If mistakes are made, who cares?! Keep playing, and keep the beat. This is what you have been practicing for—the ability to not worry, and just DO IT!

If you have played in a band or an orchestra, you know the feeling of keeping the beat, going on no matter what mistakes have been made. You can reach this stage in your piano playing, where you keep going no matter what.

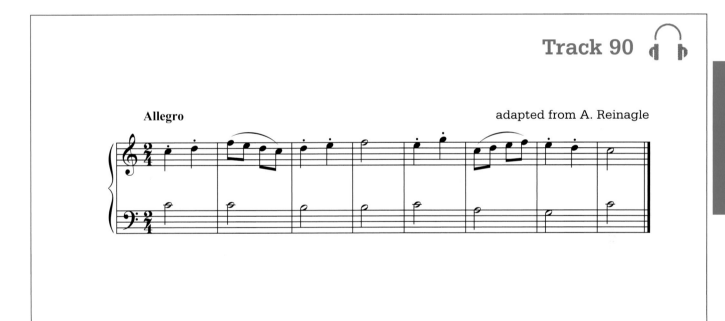

Track 90

Allegro

adapted from A. Reinagle

THE METRONOME
This will help you keep a steady beat

If you wish to play the piano "in time," the metronome can help. Invented in 1812, the mechanical metronome was made portable in 1816; Beethoven was the first well-known composer to use metronome indications in his music in 1817.

Keeping time with the metronome involves listening closely. Don't use it when you are playing a piece that you have not perfected. I suggest using it as you warm up with five-finger patterns. Set the metronome at 100 and play the pattern slowly, feeling two ticks per note. This forces you to listen for the beats. When you feel confident with two ticks per beat, go to one beat per tick. Now set the metronome to 72 and play two notes per tick. During this time you can be changing the five-finger patterns you are playing.

Metronome Types

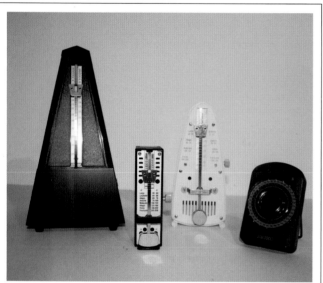

- Here are some different types and styles of metronomes.

- There is the old but beautiful pyramid shape. It is a wind up.

- A later version is encased in plastic and was meant to be more portable.

- The modern electronic one is very handy to carry with you, and fits easily in a purse or a music case.

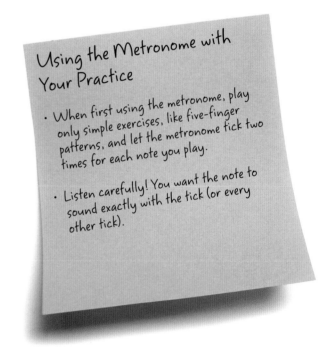

Using the Metronome with Your Practice

- When first using the metronome, play only simple exercises, like five-finger patterns, and let the metronome tick two times for each note you play.

- Listen carefully! You want the note to sound exactly with the tick (or every other tick).

When using it with a piece you have learned, choose one measure, decide on a comfortable beat to set the metronome, listen to one full measure of ticks, then play the one measure. If the piece has hands together, play only one hand. You should gauge how it feels and if you can attempt more than one measure.

Here are my suggestions for using metronome with the piece below:

Choose one measure, perhaps the first one, and play hands separately until it feels easy.

Turn the metronome to 80 and clap the right hand part with the tick, which equals a quarter note. Now play the right hand with the metronome. Always count 3 or 4 beats with the metronome before you begin.

Now play the left hand with the metronome. When this feels easy, try the measure hands together.

You can continue with each measure in the piece; then start playing two measures with the metronome.

Clementine

• This piece is here for you to work with the metronome.

EXERCISE FINGERS/HANDS/BRAIN

Read a little on the brain to find out how important and useful playing music is

It is so important for you to play as much as you can with all ten fingers. Each digit needs to play slowly and hold down its key for a couple of beats. In this way you strengthen each finger and make each one more independent. Of course, the fingers are dependent on each other, on the whole hand, on the wrist, on the arm. But each finger needs to be able to

"hold its own." There are many studies on the value to the brain of playing music. Music, even just listening actively, uses many parts of the brain. Playing the piano uses more parts of the brain than most other activities, including sports. Think about it: You read from two different clefs at the same time; the arm muscles and tendons work together and

Track 92

Country Gardens

traditional

- This is a piece with some analytical hints to help you learn it.
- How many measures are alike?
- Which notes are sharped?
- Practice the most common rhythm—♩ ♫ ♩ ♩

independently; your right foot activates the pedal; and you have to choose where in the music the pedal is used. If you think anymore about it, you won't be able to do it! I'm only kidding, but it makes me realize how much work this is, and how much automation takes place.

We all benefit from this "brain exercise." Fortunately, it is more than simply an exercise, for it involves emotions. What a wonderful way to express yourself!

In order for you to express yourself, there needs to be a certain amount of automation; by this I mean that you practice certain elements over and over until it is automatic. Only then will you feel free to express yourself through music.

So you go to your piano or electric keyboard again, to practice your exercises, study the piece you want to play, practice each hand alone, play very slowly through the piece. One day you can just play it! That is a wonderful feeling, but you must be patient.

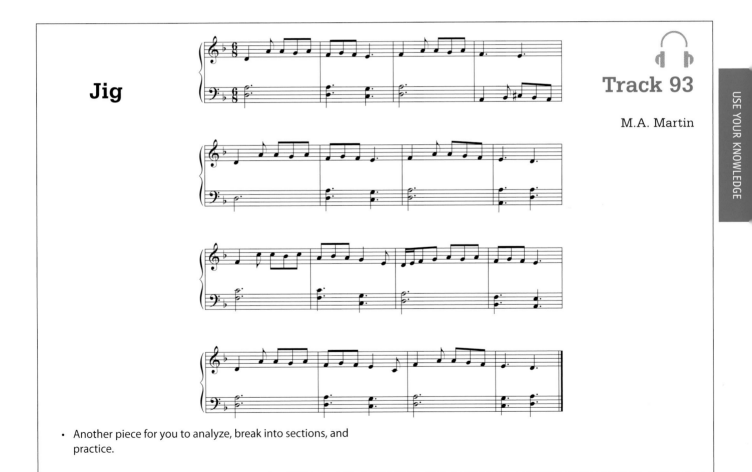

Jig

Track 93

M.A. Martin

- Another piece for you to analyze, break into sections, and practice.

MUSIC
We have analyzed and theorized, but in the end it's the music that is important

Here is your opportunity to use everything you have learned and practiced. Use your eyes and brain to see what is in the piece and what the piece is about. Use your ears and brain to tell you what is correct, what is wrong. The pieces below are in two different styles: "Oh! Susanna" is a folk song, fairly simple to remember, and sung by just about everyone.

"Allegro" is a piece written during the classical period (app. 1750–1850) by a teacher and composer, Anton Diabelli (1781–1858) who was very famous at the time. It has a simple left hand that accompanies a lovely melody.

Most classical music has a tempo and mood marking at the beginning, just above the first line on the left side. As with

Track 94

- This is the final, final production of "Oh! Susanna."

- The upbeat is now two eighth notes, so count 1-2-3 and start playing on four.

other musical terms, these are usually in Italian. The most common are: *Lento,* slowly; *adagio,* at ease or in an easy, graceful manner; *andante,* at a medium walking pace; *moderato,* at a moderate tempo; *allegro,* fast and cheerful; *vivace,* lively; *presto,* fast as possible.

There are many subdivisions of these, and if you have one, a metronome gives approximate numbers to these tempi. But choosing a correct tempo is a very subjective decision. If you listen to several recordings of the same piece you will realize how different the performances can be. It all comes down to this: What mood are you trying to project, and how easily can you play the piece at the tempo you want. You can play a piece in a lively manner, but the tempo does not have to be so fast to project the mood of liveliness. Also, your moderate tempo may be someone else's lively tempo, and yet someone else's slow tempo.

Allegro

Anton Diabelli

Track 95

- This piece notes Allegro as a tempo instruction, but you should work toward playing it correctly, in a steady, slow tempo.

- When it feels comfortable, hands together, at a slower tempo, then you can start playing it faster, but only in small increments. Always begin by playing it slowly, then a little faster each time. A metronome will be handy for this.

ARPEGGIATING A MAJOR TRIAD
You get a harp-like sound with arpeggios

Arpa is the Italian word for "harp." When you play arpeggios on the piano, you choose a chord, play one note at a time, and continue up or down the keyboard. Hold the damper pedal down for a really good harp sound!

You can cover the whole keyboard with a long arpeggio. Practice the moves by starting at the bottom, the lowest key on the piano, and build the A major triad in the left hand, an octave higher in the right hand. Play these chords blocked—you are rehearsing the moves.

Play each successive A major triad by easily and gracefully crossing left hand over right hand, then slipping right under the left hand to prepare the next chord. Play up as far as you can, then play down. Now the right hand will reverse the action by going over the left hand; the left hand will slip

A Major Triad, Both Hands

- Both hands are ready to play an A major triad.

- Since you will be playing one note at a time, practice that now, starting with the lowest note.

- When you get to the highest key in the right hand, play back down.

A Major Triad, LH Over RH

- The right hand is still on its chord.

- The left hand has crossed over to prepare another A major triad, an octave above the right hand.

- You may keep going—the right hand slips under the left hand and prepares another triad an octave above the last one.

- Play up this arpeggio (single notes) slowly, all the way to the top. Then play back down the arpeggio; this time the right hand crosses over the left hand.

under the right hand to prepare the next triad.

Now repeat all of this, but play one note at a time. Be able to name the notes in the triad, because when you descend, you have to play the top note of the triad first in each hand.

Another way to play chords, especially as an accompaniment, is to break them up into a pattern that has you playing the triad "bottom, top, middle, top." The fingering of the left hand would be, 5-1-3-1. If you play a chord in this fashion it is called an Alberti bass. When you play it you should be reminded of the music of Mozart and his contemporaries. It was used a lot in the piano music of the classical period (roughly 1750–1850).

Examples of Alberti Bass

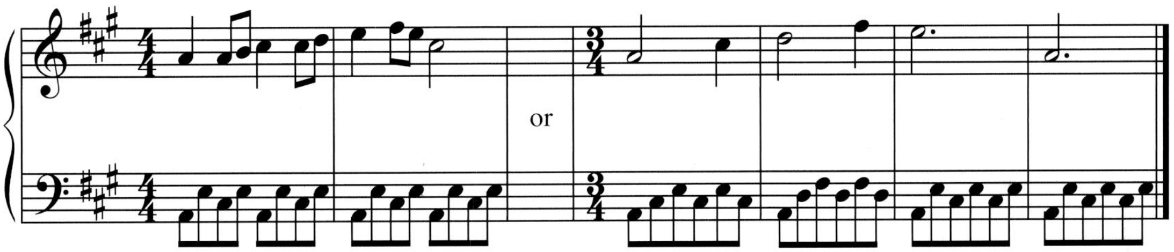

or

• The above arpeggio (the shorter version) is illustrated here.

ARPEGGIOS

MAJOR CHORD WITHIN AN OCTAVE
Four notes in each hand can make a big sound!

If your hands are fairly large, and/or there is good stretch between the fingers, you may want to try an enlarged triad. Instead of A-C♯-E with fingers 5-3-1 and 1-3-5, play A-C♯-E-A with fingers 5-3-2-1 (LH) and 1-2-3-5 (RH). Notice the intervals between the notes: a 3rd, a 3rd, then a 4th. The 4th is between the top two notes. When you invert the chord, the 4th is in the middle; and when you play the 2nd inversion the

4th is at the bottom.

Whether you can do this or not, you can certainly extend the chord one note at a time to play arpeggios. Don't concern yourself with covering every key of the chord before you begin to play. Let your wrists and arms be relaxed and flexible, but in a straight line with the finger that is playing.

Like the fingering of a scale, the third or fourth finger has

A Major Chord Extended

- Even though the model can cover all four keys with one hand, this is not a "must."

- Play one note at a time; keep wrist and arm straight with the finger that is playing.

- The arm and hand give support to the finger that plays.

A Major Chord Extended Further

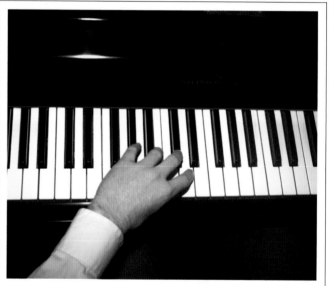

- As in a scale, the 3rd (or 4th) finger has to cross over the thumb. Of course, this is a larger motion than in a scale.

- Remember that you need to support each finger that plays. The motion you make with your arm and wrist need only do that and no more.

Track 97

216

to cross over the thumb as you continue the arpeggio up or down. In the opposite direction, the thumb must cross under the third or fourth finger.

Practice playing up and down this four-note chord; keep the arms flexible so they can support the 5th fingers when they play.

Invert this chord. Left hand 5 and right hand 1 will be on C♯; LH 4 and RH 2 play E; LH 2 and RH 4 play A; LH 1 and RH 5 play the next C♯. Play up and down this inversion, keeping your arms relaxed, and gently, subtly swinging to support the 5th fingers.

You can practice the 2nd inversion the same way. Please play one hand at a time, even though the photos and the music illustrate hands together. There is a lot to feel, hear, and think about as you play these chords.

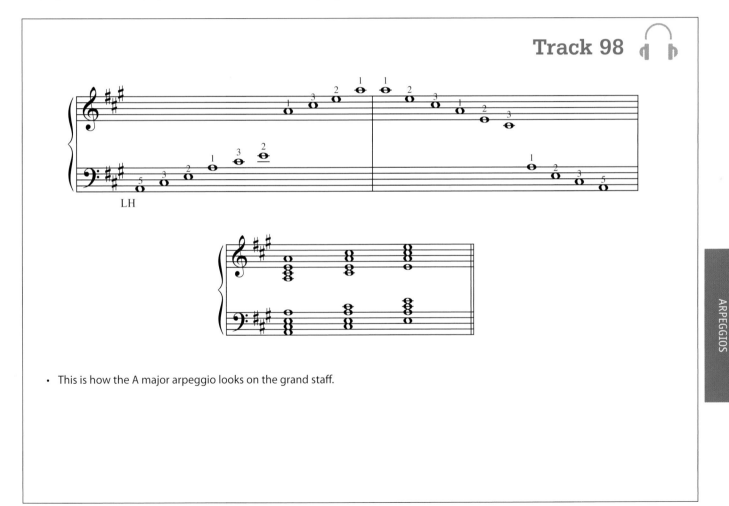

Track 98

- This is how the A major arpeggio looks on the grand staff.

ONE NOTE AT A TIME
Each note of the arpeggio carries equal weight, which means to keep the wrist straight

To practice playing the arpeggio, begin by saying the names of the notes in the chord backward and forward. As the right hand plays up the chord (start just below middle C), count three to each note (that will slow you down!), make sure the line from the playing finger to the elbow is straight, and name each key as you play it.

Play up for two octaves, ending on finger 5; then play down. Keep naming the keys! Keep counting 3 to each note so you can check for relaxation (stretch to play the key, let hand return to a small, relaxed position), for a straight line from playing finger to elbow.

Are you feeling comfortable with the arpeggio? You need

- The hand stays in a small shape.

- The elbow is out in order to keep the straight line from fingertip to elbow.

- After you play each key, make sure your hand, wrist, and arm feel relaxed. This is why your hand needs to remain in or return to its smaller shape.

- Fingers 2 and 3 are reaching toward the next notes.

- When finger 2 plays, the thumb will relax into the small shape.

- This is another good way to practice any chords. It calls

for you to really know the names of the notes in the chord.

- With this in mind, choose a different chord to arpeggiate each time you practice.

to practice it in the left hand. The same suggestions apply. Play slowly, keep each finger supported by the arm. Play up the arpeggio, crossing 3rd finger over the thumb. After two octaves, play down the arpeggio, gently sliding the thumb under the 3rd finger. Play so slowly that it must be correct (that means that you know the notes of your chord really well).

Please pay attention to your body—arms, wrists, hands, and fingers. If they are communicating, "This hurts!" you must stop, rest your hands, and then play music that requires less stretch.

Another part of the body to pay attention to is the back. If you sit at the piano for a long period of time, you may feel it in the shoulders and/or the small of the back. Be sure to take a break, stretch, lie on the floor, in order to relax the back muscles. Those muscles must be trained for stamina, as well as the hands!

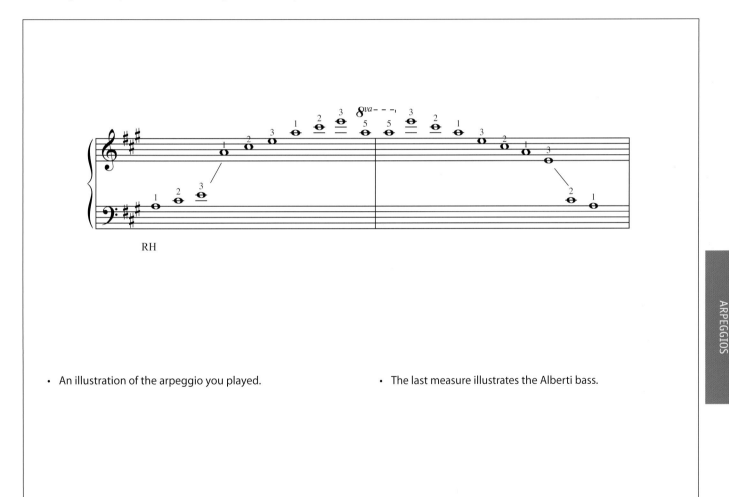

- An illustration of the arpeggio you played.

- The last measure illustrates the Alberti bass.

EQUAL TIME: LEFT HAND
The left hand can use those wonderful, rich bass tones on the piano

The right hand has conquered the arpeggio; the left hand is developing its technique. Use the same process; i.e., name the notes of the chord backward and forward; as you play up the arpeggio, count three to each key and name the key. Keep a small hand shape as you reach for the next key—a straight line from the fingertip that is playing, to the elbow.

Right and left hands can play the arpeggio at the same time, an octave apart. Both thumbs play at the same time, in many arpeggios, which makes playing the arpeggio hands together a little easier.

Also, you can play the inversions fairly easily hands together, slowly. There is no need for you to play the arpeggio fast.

- A piece that uses the newly practiced arpeggio.

Playing arpeggios, either with each hand or both hands, gives you another method of moving about the keyboard freely. It also gives you a stretch between all the fingers, and yet another muscle memory that reoccurs throughout your music.

After you feel comfortable with the arpeggio in the left hand, go through the steps mentioned before for the right hand: invert the chord and play the arpeggio up and down from another note in the chord; break the triad into an Alberti bass pattern, 5-1-3-1, then invert the triad and use the easiest fingering for playing the Alberti pattern (for left hand, 5-1-3-1 for the first inversion, 5-1-2-1 for the second inversion).

Another excellent accompaniment pattern for the left hand is to play up and down the chord: G-B-D-G-D-B-G. The left hand pinky starts on a lower G; then finger 3 (or 4) on B, finger 2 on D, finger 1 on the next G (one octave above the first G). You can change chords quickly by playing, for instance, G-C-E-G-E-C-G.

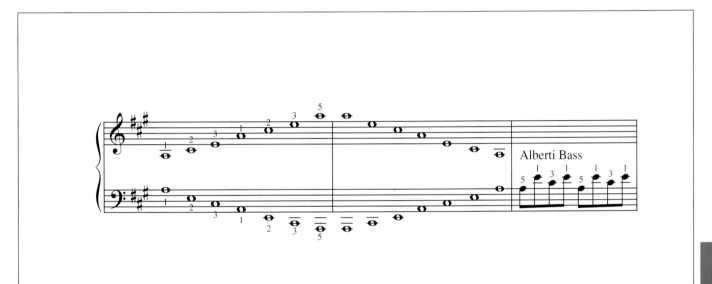

- The A major arpeggio written out for both hands. You can go in opposite directions fairly easily.

- The last measure illustrates the Alberti bass.

OPEN-CHORD ACCOMPANIMENT
Skip a chord note, spread out the arpeggio, for a romantic sound

Don't you wonder how the pianist makes those romantic-sounding piano accompaniments? It is a kind of arpeggio, but different in that a chord note is skipped and placed above the 5th of the chord. This is called an open chord. Press down the damper pedal and try playing this open chord, one note at a time. The right hand can continue the chord in close position: after the LH has played low D, 2nd finger

on A, thumb on F#, the RH plays just above the F# on A, then D, then F#. When I hear this accompaniment pattern, I think of an accompaniment figure for "Send in the Clowns," but it could be for any ballad.

On the classical side, there are Chopin nocturnes. Each of his nocturnes has a different kind of open-chord left hand part, or there is simply a bass note and chord as the pattern.

D Major Open Chord, LH

- Use the 2nd finger of the LH as a pivot to swing the arm and thumb toward the F♯. It is a slow motion; don't rush it.

- Practice playing the interval of a 5th, fingers 5 to 2, keeping the hand small by letting go of the pinky.

D Major Open Chord, LH

- Finish the "swing" through the pivot finger 2, to thumb on F♯.

- Keeping arm and wrist relaxed, practice the open chord from low D, through pivot key, A, up to F♯, back and forth.

- When it feels easy, press down the damper pedal and play it again, either up and down, or just ascending.

Most of these songs and instrumental pieces have a middle section that contrasts with the first and last section (which are basically the same with some differences). In classical music, these sections are labeled A-B-A. In popular music, the middle section is usually called a "bridge."

Try this open-chord pattern with other chords, with and without black keys.

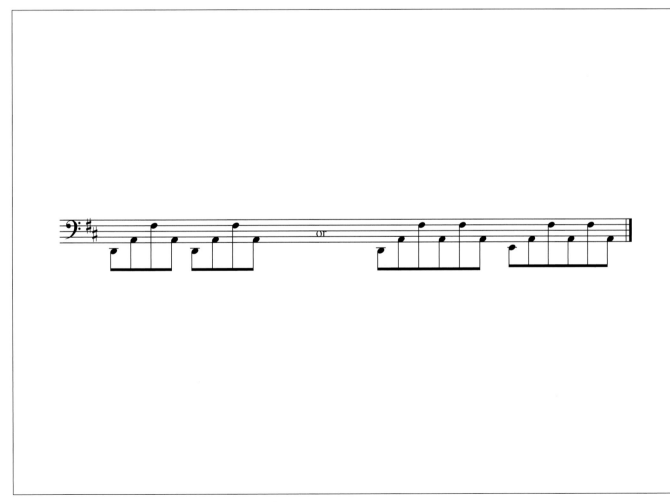

ARPEGGIOS

MUSIC
Accompany beautiful melodies with flowing, open chords

Some guitar books have just the melody and words of a song, and chord symbols over the staff. If you are interested in making your own accompaniments, this kind of book is a good alternative to piano books. You will need to make a more in-depth study of different kinds of chords, and there are books that teach you about that. Songs with the melody written out, but not the left hand part (chord symbols over the staff) are called "lead sheets." Fake books are simply compilations of lead sheets.

Listen to popular music from recent musicals, and ballad-type popular songs; most of these have flowing accompaniments, whether on the guitar or on the keyboard. Purchase

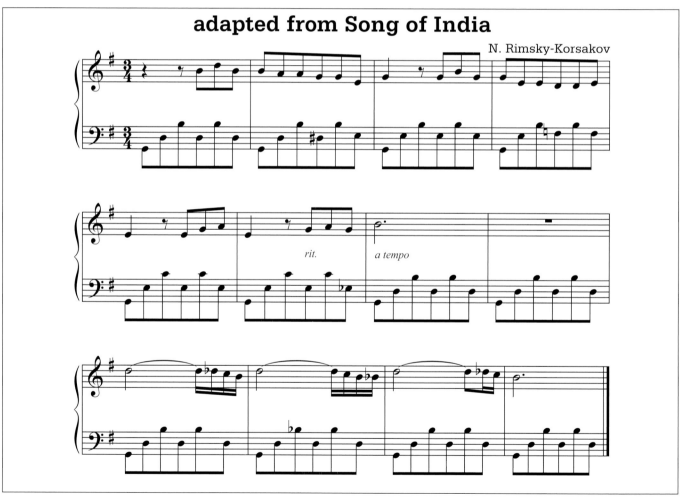

adapted from Song of India

N. Rimsky-Korsakov

a book of songs/music you want to play. You can practice either the piano part written in the music, or you can play the melody in the right hand and make up your own accompaniments. Use all the ideas you have learned about analyzing and practicing.

When you reach a dead end and can't seem to get anywhere, find a private piano teacher. Usually a teacher is willing to give one or two lessons to help you over a "hump." Look for resources at the local music store or music school.

The people there can recommend teachers, or they can recommend classes in which you can enroll.

Music is a life-long study, even for professional musicians. There are so many musical ways in which you can express yourself, it feels somewhat daunting to choose which area you wish to study. But then, you can study them all!

Keep your eyes on the prize—being able to express yourself by playing an instrument easily and freely. Enjoy the process of getting to that point.

ARPEGGIOS

BOOKS

RESOURCES

Adult Piano Method: Lessons, Solos, Technique and Theory by Fred
 Kern, Phillip Keveren, Barbara Kreader, and Mona Rejino
Published by Hal Leonard

There are scads of adult piano method books, and it would serve
 the reader well if he/she made an investigation of available
 materials. But as a teacher, this one book (with two CDs) is my
 choice for the first book for any adult beginner. It uses all the steps
 I use for a beginner, and it is laid out beautifully. The CDs are also
 excellent.

Keyboard Musician for the Adult Beginner by Frances Clark, Louise
 Goss, and Roger Grove
Published by Summy-Birchard

This is the first adult piano method book I used, and it is by my idol
 in piano teaching: Frances Clark. I use her method, The Music Tree,
 for children, and this book uses the same construction and order
 but moves faster. The pros for this book include the excellent
 selection of repertoire throughout. The cons are: it moves really
 fast, and the print is too small.

Musicophilia: Tales of Music and the Brain by Oliver Sacks
Published by Vintage Books/Random House

This is a wonderful set of stories that relate the effect of music on
 the brain. There is something for everyone in this book! It enlight-
 ens us on the importance of studying music, for the health of our
 brains as well as our souls.

The Piano by John-Paul Williams
Published by Crown Publishing Group

I don't have this book, but the synopsis and advertisement on the
 Barnes and Noble Web site make it look very appealing. It includes
 a complete history, and how to care for the instrument, with lots
 of beautiful color photos.

The Piano Book: Buying and Owning a New or Used Piano by Larry Fine
Published by Brookside Press (there should also be an *Annual Supplement to the Piano Book*)

I have a well-worn copy of this book. It is a practical guide on everything about the acoustic piano—how it is made, the different models and how they vary, anything you ever wanted to know about your piano, or one that you are considering buying.

Speaking of Pianists by Abram Chasins
Published by Da Capo Press

This is a good book to start reading anywhere. There are lots of conversational stories about professional pianists. You can buy an inexpensive used copy on Amazon.com.

MAGAZINES

Piano Today

A quarterly publication catering to lovers and players of classical and jazz piano music. There are workshop articles in rhythm, harmony, and jazz stylings, usually at an intermediate to advanced level.
2 Depot Plaza
Bedford Hill, NY 10507
www.pianotoday.com

Pianist

Published six times a year, in England, this magazine is accompanied by a CD in each issue. Scores for the music on the CD are in the magazine. There are usually a couple of duet pieces, and an informative "Keyboard Class," which explains things like lead sheets and chord charts. There is also a Q and A column for amateur pianists.

I have found this a very good magazine for amateurs, and well worth the money for a subscription from England.
www.expressmag.com
email: expsmag@expressmag.com

Clavier Companion

A recent merger of *Clavier* magazine and *Keyboard Companion*, this is a publication for teachers, professional musicians, and for amateurs who want more from a piano magazine. The advantage for the beginning pianist is that the forums are for teachers of beginner and intermediate students. There are always good articles for the ambitious adult beginner. It is published bi-monthly by the Frances Clark Center for Keyboard Pedagogy
90 Main Street
P.O. Box 651
Kingston, NJ 08528
Email: claviercompanion@pfsmag.com

SCHOOLS & ORGANIZATIONS

Schools

There are community music schools in many areas of the country. If there is not one near you, then go to the local music store. Many of them have teachers of piano and other instruments.

Organizations

Music Teachers National Association

MTNA is an organization for professional musicians and teachers. Their Web site is

www.mtna.org

National Music Certificate Program

NMCP runs a testing program throughout the United States. There is a practical test and a theory test, given at centers around the country. The judges are well trained and well qualified. The syllabus that is given to each teacher-member contains an excellent selection of repertoire, including pop/jazz pieces. Adults are welcome at any level, but you need a teacher to enter the testing program.

P.O. Box 1984

Buffalo, NY 14240-1984

www.nationalmusiccertificate.org

National Federation of Music Clubs

This organization has been around since the latter part of the nineteenth century. They promote the study of music, and provide opportunities for young people to perform and earn awards and prizes throughout the country.

www.nfmc-music.org

WEB SITES

Fundamentals of Piano Practice

An interesting Web site for practice ideas. Most of the ideas are sound, but there is a lot of "talk" which makes it seem too verbose. It is definitely worth exploring.

www.pianofundamentals.com

Gary Ewer's Easy Music Theory

I have subscribed to this free newsletter for a couple of years and found different ways of testing knowledge of music theory, and different ways to present music basics to students.

www.musictheory.halifax.ns.ca

Reviews Nest

When I type in "piano lessons" on my computer, I am deluged with Web sites for piano lessons, many offered free (for one lesson). I was greatly helped by the Web site, "Reviewsnest/pianolessons." They review the piano lesson Web sites and present you with their reviews and preferences. They are labeled for age and range levels, and ease of ordering (plus the price). I would recommend visiting the site for help in finding an appropriate lesson program.

www.reviewsnest.com/PianoLessons

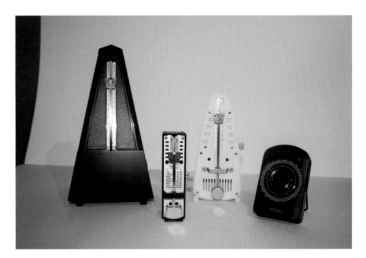

GLOSSARY

Accelerando: Play gradually faster.

Allegro: Literally, it means "cheerful." For musicians it means a lively tempo.

Andante: A relaxed, walking tempo.

Arpeggio: An extended broken chord; it can be as short as 3 or 4 notes, or cover the whole keyboard.

Chord: Several notes which sound harmonious, or pleasant, played at the same time (blocked) or one note at a time (broken)

Contrary Motion: Two voices (or hands) go in opposite directions.

Crescendo: Get gradually louder.

Damper pedal: The right foot pedal; when pressed down with the right foot, the dampers lift off the strings, allowing them to vibrate longer.

D.C. al Fine: An indication at the end of a piece of music that means to go back to the beginning and play to the end (da capo al Fine).

Decrescendo: Get gradually softer.

Downbeat: the first beat in a measure.

Dynamics: How softly or loudly to play.

Enharmonic: Two notes (or one key) sound the same, but have different names.

Fallboard: The board that covers the piano keys, or folds back to uncover the keys.

Flat (♭): Written before the note, it means to play the very next key (either black or white) lower, or to the left.

Forte (F): Play loudly.

Fortissimo (FF): Play very loudly.

Grand staff: Two staffs, usually a treble staff and a bass staff, connected by a brace. Used for any keyboard music.

Interval: The distance from one pitch (note) to another pitch (note)

Key Signature: A series of sharp or flat symbols placed on the staff designating consistent changes throughout the music.

Legato: To play smoothly with no break in sound.

Lento: To play at a slow tempo.

Measures: The way music is organized so that rhythm is easier to read. Measures are separated by bar lines.

Metronome: A device for keeping a steady pulse. It ticks like a clock, to a rate of 40 beats per minute up to 208 beats per minute.

Natural sign(♮): Cancels a sharp or flat.

P5th: An abbreviation used in this book for perfect 5th. There should be six keys between the notes.

Parallel motion: Two voices (or hands) move in the same direction.

Passing tones or notes: In a melody, the notes between chord tones.

Phrase: A musical sentence or phrase, often recognized by a slur over the notes.

Pianissimo (PP): Play very softly.

Piano (P): Play softly.

Ritardando: (abbreviated *rit.*) Gradually slow down the tempo.

Scale: A series of notes that are consecutive in the musical alphabet.

Sharp (#): Written before a note, it means to play the very next key (either black or white) higher, or to the right.

Slur: A curved line over or under a group of notes, which indicates to play smoothly (legato).

Staccato: A dot over or under a note that indicates to play detached.

Syncopation: moving strong beats to a weak beat placement, and vice versa.

Tempo: The speed at which the basic beat moves.

Tie: A curved line connecting two notes of the same pitch. The sound lasts as long as the two notes together.

Time signature: Numbers at the beginning of a piece, one on top of the other. The top number indicates how many beats, or pulses, are in each measure; the bottom number is a symbol for the kind of note that equals one beat, or pulse.

Tonic: The first degree of a scale; the "home" key [of a piece of music].

Triad: A chord with three different notes.

Upbeat: A note, or notes, which comes before the first full measure of a piece.

INDEX

INDEX

INDEX

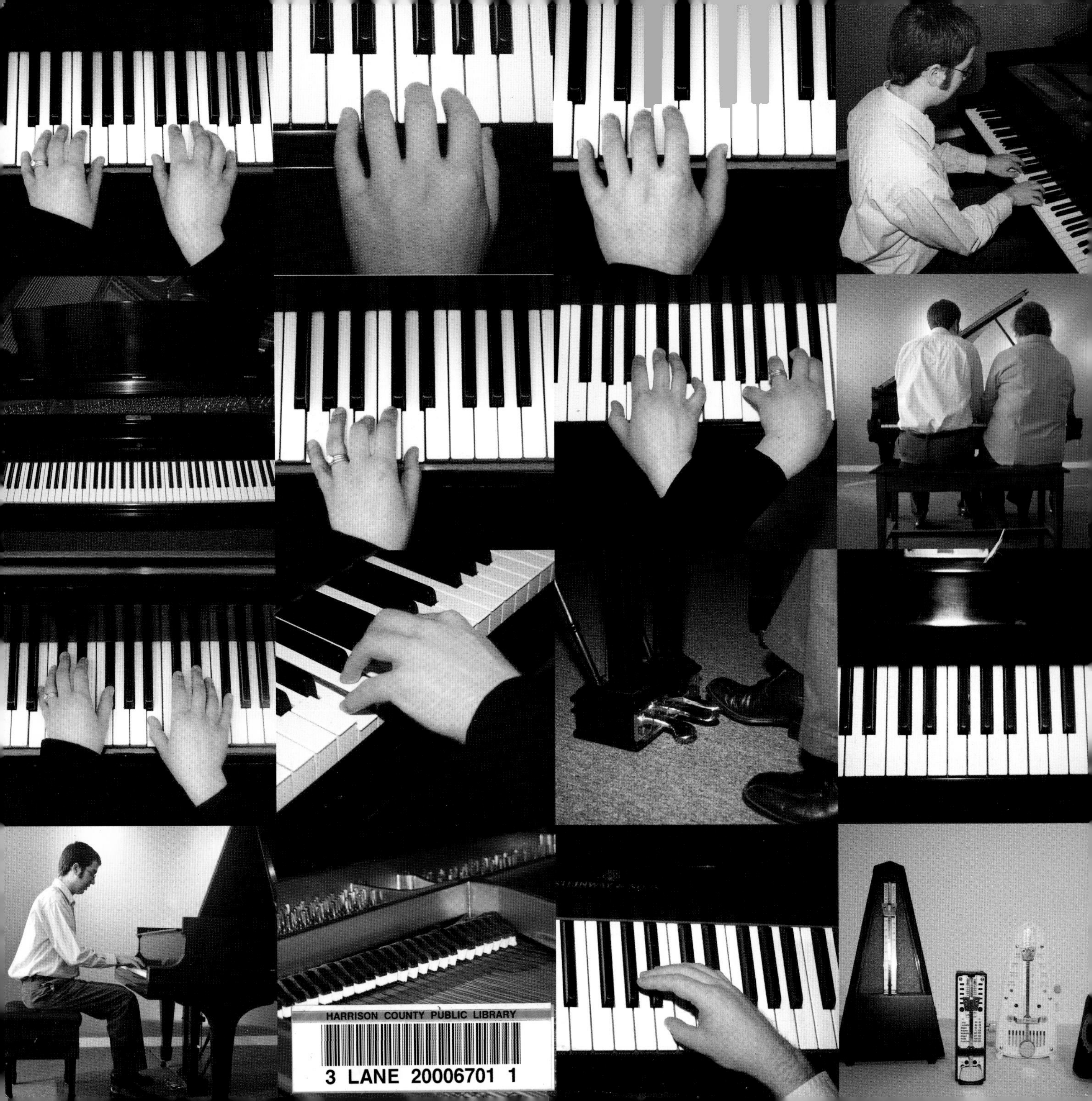